How to Demonstrate

Effective Leadership

How to Demonstrate

Effective
Leadership

24 Real-Life Examples of Grace in Action

Kennedy A. Germain

Published by Germain Empowerment
https://germainempowerment.com

This book is dedicated to:

My mom, my prayer warrior, who taught me that the Hand of God in my life was better than all the riches in this world;

My dad, my hero, who sacrificed so much for me to enjoy the blessings of God that are chasing me down;

My wife, my love and spiritual partner, who keeps me grounded and always reminds me that God is in control;

My children, my legacy, who represent the true Grace of God in my life

Acknowledgements

I would like to thank the many people who brought me to this journey. First, Mr. Rommel Lawrence, my high school English teacher at Saint Mary's Academy, for raising the writer from within me and encouraging me to document and sell my first work, *As We Pondered*, a booklet of poems I co-authored with my friend Eddie Toulon, published by the St. Mary's Academy in the Commonwealth of Dominica.

I would like to thank my cousin, Giftus John, for being my inspiration and support in writing. Multi-talented-all-things-artsy (photography, oil painting, poetry), Giftus is the author of the following books: *The Island Man Sings His Song, Mesye Kwik-Kwak, Ma Williams and Her Circle of Friends, Verses from Atop the Mountain, Ma Williams: The Story of Love and Family, Quarantined, Two Weeks One Summer*, and *Voices of Lamentation*.

Thank you to my many family and friends who spoke positive words into my life and encouraged me on this journey. A special thank you to my family: my life partner, Junie, my chief cheerleader who keeps me grounded in life and faith; my daughter, Jacqui, who is a literary genius and author of the book *When the Ghosts Come*

Ashore, as well as an inspiration to me; Gordon and Lincoln for their encouragement and role modeling of true leadership in their respective organizations. Thank you to my son and mini-me (well, he is not "mini" anymore), Kevin, whom I admire as a pillar of strength; Al for his perpetual positive energy; Johnson and Gairy for being there and believing in me; and Matty and Lin for allowing me to pour into their lives and for reciprocating love into mine. And thank you to my mom and dad, my rock and support, who had me reading my written work over the radio airwaves as a child in Dominica because they believed that my written and spoken words were a blessing to others.

Thanks to my first manuscript readers, Alison Main, Monique Picou, Karan Langham Dyson, Bonnie Curtis, Bruce Simeone, and L'Tanya Cole, whose leadership I emulated, and to coaches Kimberly Adkins, author of *Empowering Women to Walk in God's Glory*; Pamela Scott-Goines, author of *Autistic and Thriving*; and Dwylett Chambers-Montgomery, author and founder of *Kids' Reality Books*.

Finally, thank you to my mentors, coaches, and sponsors who provided the support needed to enjoy a great and successful professional career. The P&G support systems within the Fabric & Home Care Black Managers Leadership Team (F&HC BMLT) with a special call-out to the Black Women Managers Initiative (BWMI), the P&G African-American Leadership Network (AALN), and the Tuskegee University Alumni Team indeed provided the platform I needed to thrive.

Thank you! Thank you! Thank you!

Praise Reviews for

How to Demonstrate Effective Leadership

How to Demonstrate Effective Leadership is an inspiring work full of practical insights about how to lead successfully with your heart, hands, and head. Kennedy shares his deep wisdom gained from many years as a faithful Christ follower and thoughtful leader in a large multinational company. The connections Kennedy makes between faith and work reveal the power of trusting God in every aspect of life and serving others to achieve outcomes beyond your wildest dreams.

Dr. Alison Main
Senior Director of Research & Development, Procter & Gamble

I have worked with Kennedy for 8 years, and during that time, our relationship has evolved into true friendship. Kennedy's own grace, as well as his determination and passion for learning, have produced a book that is full of important leadership tips, real-life examples, and inspiration. *How to Demonstrate Effective Leadership* is a readable and enlightening book.

Bonnie Curtis
Chief Human Resources Officer, Castellini Group

The author, Mr. Kennedy, has taken solid leadership principles, related them to points in scripture, and demonstrated the execution with real-life examples, making this a unique book. From cover to cover, it is easy to understand and straightforward. The result is a fun reading experience, while making every principle a teaching moment on many levels. Imagine that! A fun leadership manual. Bravo!

Bruce
Retired P&G Manufacturing Manager

I have read many books on leadership, but I have not read many addressing leadership from a Biblical perspective. It is easy to think that successes in our professions are a matter of luck and determined solely by our hard work and being in the right place at the right time, and we fail to consider that these outcomes might have been influenced by something beyond us. Kennedy makes a compelling case that some of the most proven leadership principles are deeply rooted in Biblical doctrine, and he has masterfully illustrated these parallels by taking the reader through a journey of his 30-plus-year career at Procter & Gamble, describing how it was positively influenced by God's Grace. It is a must-read for business leaders at various stages of their careers and will certainly cause one to reevaluate their leadership style and truly uncover what it takes to be a great leader.

V. Gordon Julien
Country Manager, St. Lucia, Republic Bank (EC) Limited

This book really spoke to me! It captured all of the things that are so important to be an exceptional leader. I absolutely loved how the book connected leadership attributes to Biblical scriptures. So often, as leaders, we are expected to check our religion at the door, but what this book clearly acknowledges is the value of spiritual behaviors in a leader. I'm looking forward to integrating these faith-based strategies as tools in developing executives within my company.

Karan Dyson
Vice President of Global Grooming Process & Engineering,
Procter & Gamble

Kennedy Germain's *How to Demonstrate Effective Leadership* is an amazing and inspirational capture of the key traits of a great leader. Kennedy has done a masterful job linking these traits back to Biblical doctrine in a way that is entertaining and easy to follow. The examples provided bring to life how he overcame some of the major challenges he faced in his long and storied career at Procter & Gamble and how he overcame them while maintaining focus on the Almighty as his North Star. *How to Demonstrate Effective Leadership* is an exceptional reference book for leaders wanting to supercharge their leadership skills, as well as a foresightful gift for graduates seeking a firm foundation and long-term guidance for their careers. This ground-breaking book is a first of its kind and a must-read for leaders and business professionals who are inspired by faith.

Lincoln D. Germain
Chief Commercial Officer, Zymergen

Kennedy does a masterful job in *How to Demonstrate Effective Leadership* connecting relevant and powerful scriptures to the critical skills required to be an effective leader. I am inspired to get even closer to God's Word and His teachings for my life's pursuits. The examples shared that parallel Kennedy's personal work experiences provide an interesting perspective into his life, connection to God, and his personal passion to engage, help, and support people. You will emerge with clear guidance on how to be a great Godly leader with a never-ending passion for success—people success, project success, and company success.

L'Tanya Q. Cole
Retired P&G Director of Global Engineering

The pages speak from the intermingling of wisdom and experience. They are practical and thoughtful. For those you are ready to receive, this is a whole meal of professional wisdom!

Monique Picou
Corporate Executive (P&G Alumni)

I loved the demonstrated examples of *How to Demonstrate Effective Leadership* and the scripture used in prayer for each situation. The examples showed the authority, boldness, integrity, and, ultimately, triumph that God gives believers in all kinds of situations throughout our careers.

Pamela Scott-Goines
Director of Student Success, Accessible Resources at
the University of Cincinnati
Author of *Autistic and Thriving*

Table of Contents

Foreword

Grace ignites leadership. Not only have I experienced this, but I have also witnessed it in the life of my friend, Kennedy Germain. For this reason, it is my distinct privilege to introduce you to the person I know and the leader I admire.

It is fascinating to me how leadership is the same, regardless of where a person leads. Whether leading in a business or a nonprofit organization such as a church, leadership is defined the same. Leadership is influence. Without influence, no one follows. More importantly, without followers, there's no leader. Although we may be tempted to focus on the need for followers, I venture to say it is far more significant to nurture the quality of our influence.

In the case of Kennedy, he led for more than three decades in the corporate world while working for the largest multinational producer of consumer goods, the Procter & Gamble Company. He was an influential figure in numerous projects and business dealings. And although his career is remarkable, his humility will not allow him to boast of the number of recognitions and accolades he collected over a thirty-year span. But even as impressive as his career is, the quality of his leadership is truly awe-inspiring.

I have met very few people who believe and live up to the principle that *who they are* and *what they do* are two distinct and separate things. Thankfully, Kennedy knows the difference. It is one of life's greatest temptations to equate our professions with our identities. As a pastor, I get to preach about the love and goodness of God while helping others discover their God-given identities in Christ. I believe that gaining awareness of who God created you to be will release you to fulfill the purpose for which you were created. It's a dangerous mission to pursue noteworthy works without awareness of your identity. You have the potential for limitless impact when you discover that simple yet powerful key.

I am convinced that Kennedy's awareness of his identity in Christ is the foundation of everything he does. He has never esteemed his career above his service in his local church. To this day, he continues to serve to the full extent of his abilities, gifts, and talents. Although many speak of servant leadership, few take up that mantle. Nonetheless, the few that serve discover the richness of the unmerited favor of God. Kennedy uncovered this favor while serving wholeheartedly, and it is this favor that inspired him as a leader and that led him to write this book.

Dear reader, I am excited for your journey as you travel through the pages of this book. I am happy and proud to recommend Kennedy as your guide. I ask God to reveal His immeasurable Grace that is available to you. I believe that this revelation will inspire you to lead by Grace.

I believe that as you explore the characteristics of a great leader, as shared in the chapters of this book, you will discover the ways God has been at work in your life—calling you and developing you for leadership. *How to Demonstrate Effective Leadership: 24 Real-Life Examples of Grace in Action* is more than a title; it is a challenge. If you are holding this book, it is because you are stepping up to that challenge and answering the call.

Eric Petree

Lead Pastor of Citygate Church

Author of *Limitless: Defy the Ordinary*

Preface

What is the meaning of Grace? According to Google's dictionary, Oxford Languages, grace is:

noun

- simple elegance or refinement of movement.

- (in Christian belief) the free and unmerited favor of God, as manifested in the salvation of sinners and the bestowal of blessings.

verb

- do honor or credit to (someone or something) by one's presence.

The focus of this book is on the latter definition for the noun form. Too often, we attribute our successes to "luck" or "chance" when, in reality, it could just be the favor of God in our lives. Recognizing God's favor changes how you view your life and frees you up to appreciate His hand in your life. Instead of depending on luck or your "blood and sweat," walking close to God allows Him to intervene by opening doors (Chapter 5: Be True to Your Word), making a path (Chapter 13: 78% Done is Better than 100% Perfect), or tearing down walls (Chapter 1: Build Bridges, Not Walls) to get you to a successful outcome. As a leader, placing your trust in God gives you a competitive advantage. It is called God's Grace. That competitive advantage will enable you to be a better person and demonstrate the characteristics of a great leader. Each chapter in *How to Demonstrate Effective Leadership* focuses on one of these characteristics.

I was on a flight from Stuttgart, Germany, to Cincinnati, Ohio, after an extremely successful trip, which I could only believe was a miracle. I should have been invited to the event but was not given the same priority as my peers and was not told about it. That was until a set of unplanned circumstances rewarded me with an invitation to—and even an award at—that event.

I was thinking of how incredibly these circumstances fell into place. I thought about the surprise award (and standing ovation) I was given for my contribution to that business. I also thought about how I was able to make a huge impact during the event. When I'm battling jetlag on my way back to the US from an international location like Asia or Europe, I usually spend more time awake than asleep during my flights. So, on this particular flight, I pulled out the brand-new journal I was given at the Stuttgart event and started writing about how it had all come together. I came to one conclusion: God had granted me much unmerited favor. It was not luck. It was not chance. It was not because I was such an expert.

The more I thought about my situation, the more I realized how much God had blessed me throughout my career with a gift of favor, which I did not deserve and could not earn: Grace. In case you are wondering, I knew I had been blessed and led by God. I just couldn't remember spending focused time thinking specifically about how God's Grace had helped me demonstrate great leadership skills.

Grace is God's favor shown to us, who don't deserve it. It is a demonstration of God's unconditional love for us. If God looked into my heart to give me what I deserved, all he would see is a mess and wickedness.

"The heart is deceitful above all things And it is extremely sick; Who can understand it fully and know its secret motives?" Jeremiah 17:9 (AMP)

The Word of God reminds me that His Grace is all I need. *2 Corinthians 12:9 (AMP) says, "But He has said to me, 'My Grace is sufficient for you [My lovingkindness and My mercy are more than enough—always available—regardless of the situation].'"* So, there I was, in the comforts of business class flying at 32,000 feet above sea level, pondering the Grace of God in my life, particularly in spite of the challenges I had experienced. It was unfortunate I had not been given the same priority as my peers, but it had all worked to my benefit in the end.

Unfortunate circumstances have a way of pushing us closer to God. Sometimes, God allows these situations to make us stronger. If your focus is fixed on God, it does not matter what the circumstances are. God will always come through for you. God turns bad into your favor! Just look at Joseph, who was thrown into prison unjustly. Even in prison, God granted him favor.

"And when Joseph's master heard the words of his wife, saying, 'This is the way your servant treated me,' his anger burned. So Joseph's master took him and put him in the prison, a place where the king's prisoners were confined; so he was there in the prison. But the Lord was with Joseph and extended lovingkindness to him, and gave him favor in the sight of the warden. The warden committed to Joseph's care (management) all the prisoners who were in the prison; so that whatever was done there, he was in charge of it. The warden paid no attention to anything that was in Joseph's care because the Lord was with him; whatever Joseph did, the Lord made to prosper." Genesis 39:19–23 (AMP)

The awareness of God's grace (unmerited favor) changed my perspective on the drivers of my successful career. To be clear, God does not play "favorites." His favor is unlocked when you follow His principles. For example, *Luke 6:38 (AMP) reads, "Give, and it will be given to you. They will pour into your lap a good measure—pressed down, shaken together, and running over [with no space left for more]."* This means that if you give of your gifts to God, He will cause others to pour into you—and not just in finances but time and talents as well. Others will favor you with blessings. This is often referred to as "the law of sowing and harvesting." When you plant a seed, you harvest more than that one seed you planted. Being obedient to God's Word will bring His favor upon your life.

My life revolves around helping others. As such, my intent for capturing this collection of my experiences of God's favor on my life is three-fold. First, I am humbly acknowledging the Grace of

God in my life. *"But he gives us more grace. That is why Scripture says: 'God opposes the proud but shows favor to the humble.'" James 4:6 (NIV).* Second, I share this to help you become more aware of the Hand of the Supernatural Power of God in your life as a leader and to recognize through your own experiences how He has been helping you—and if you don't have that relationship with Him, how you can turn that around to give you a competitive advantage. In other words, I would like to be a blessing to you and, hopefully, influence a positive difference in your life. Of course, if this all sounds foreign to you, you can get to know that great God and receive His gift freely. That same Grace can save you from eternal separation from His love. *"For it is by grace you have been saved, through faith—and this is not from yourselves, it is the gift of God." Ephesians 2:8 (NIV).*

Third, this book is meant to provide you with a cache of real-life experiences of the application of various leadership skills. It is for those who are seeing their mentors and leadership coaches—who happen to be Baby Boomers—retire and take their mentoring with them. It is for those who are told to demonstrate more "leadership" but given only vague explanations of what that means.

In my more than three decades of corporate experience at the Procter & Gamble Company, the greatest leaders I knew demonstrated great empathy and care for others. They had the heart of servant leaders and were not boastful or prideful. Instead, they seemed to feel blessed for their positions and were greatly motivated to help others. They are the kinds of leaders anyone would want to follow—and not out of obligation but because they would want to. They were my role models, influencers of my leadership style.

At the end of my awesome corporate career, I was humbled by the great outpouring of love at my retirement celebrations by so many who said that I'd had a great influence on their lives. I actually believe it was the other way around. It was *they* who touched *me* and had allowed God to use them to enable my success in ways I alone could not do. As such, this capture of my experiences and successes reflects the true architect of my success: the Hand of God in my life, which shone through the characteristics of me as a business leader.

I hope you find *How to Demonstrate Effective Leadership* informative and the principles helpful in honing your own leadership skills. Great leaders never stop learning and instead continue refreshing themselves.

Far better than being a great leader is being a child of God.

"For whoever finds Me (Wisdom) finds life And obtains favor and grace from the Lord." Proverbs 8:35 (AMP)

DISCLAIMER: To protect the individuals mentioned, no real individual, project, or business unit names have been used in this book. The names of most functions and most actual locations have also been modified to conceal the real locations. My experiences, however, were very real.

Introduction

When I was young, I was a competitive, success-hungry young manager who was constantly being told I needed to improve my leadership skills. Being an African American, I later got some additional context to that feedback, but that's for my next book. However, this drove me to take many leadership classes. I read many leadership books. I listened to many presentations. I was fired up! I had to shed the perception that I was not a leader. This all worked fine and dandy until I would get into a real-life struggle with a difficult communication situation, as an example, and it would not be long before my confidence walls would crumble. After the dust settled, my sky-high blood pressure dropped, and the deep furrows of unhappiness that were plastered on my face disappeared, I would contemplate why the examples I learned in a communication skills class did not fit my unique and challenging situation. Somehow, when the going got tough, I did not have real examples to replicate. The case studies I learned did not apply to me. I needed some real-life examples that I could use as guides. Welcome to *How to Demonstrate Effective Leadership: 24 Real-Life Examples of Grace in Action*.

How to Demonstrate Effective Leadership is not your typical leadership book. It is not an eloquent capture of the in-depth and detailed theories of the various leadership skills. There are many books that already do that. Did I hear a sigh of relief? Great! But I do start with an overview of each leadership skill before taking you on a journey of how I have been able to apply that particular skill. You will find a strong focus on the demonstration of the application of various leadership skills. You will also find some skills applied in a different way from your paradigm. For example, when you think about a leader caring, you don't necessarily think of standing up to fight for someone. Yet, that's one great way leaders demonstrate that they care and support their people.

This book is structured in a way that conveys spiritual linkages that you don't need to be a religious scholar to understand and appreciate. It underscores the point that God's Grace opens doors for us to be successful. There are three sections that convey a collection of skills that will enable you to be a 360-degree leader if you apply them. Also, each chapter is crowned by a relevant scripture and ends with lessons learned from the application of that skill. You can read each chapter individually, or you can focus on a single section to strengthen those particular skills.

As you read this book, you will:

- Learn through real-life examples how to apply various leadership skills

- Learn some alternate applications of these skills versus conventional approaches

- Appreciate the spiritual approach to being a successful leader

- Understand the context, reflect, and see the Hand of God in your life

- Learn from the wide variety of experiences for a broader perspective

- Benefit from the helpful resources added as a bonus at the end of the book in the form of questions for reflection, a memory jogger model, and a scenario guide to aid with on-the-spot application

How to Demonstrate Effective Leadership is your handy resource guide.

Section I
Leading with Your Heart

Chapter 1

Build Bridges

Power Scripture:

How good and pleasant it is when God's people live together in unity!

Psalms 133:1 (NIV)

Relationship-Building

Strong relationship-building skills separate great leaders from the rest. The foundation is having good interpersonal skills. This means being able to work through issues, solve challenges, give feedback, and, all the while, leave no dead bodies behind.

You cannot be a servant leader (having the objective to serve others) without strong interpersonal skills. The ability to build relationships not only builds bridges instead of walls, but it also enables collaboration for faster results. Healthy relationships are trusting, honest, supportive, mutually beneficial, and strategic, among other characteristics.

On the other hand, there are many destroyers of healthy relationships. One example is being egocentric. It drives selfishness, wanting to always appear on top of your game and not let others see you work hard, always being defensive instead of taking accountability, and never showing any capacity for emotional vulnerability. One of the biggest destroyers is a one-sided relationship. A relationship that only benefits you makes you a parasite. Of course, I need not mention that advancing a business relationship into one that is inappropriate is harmful to everyone involved.

A relationship builder understands that 1 + 1 = 3, and together, we can get more done than we can on our own. Investing in relationships, therefore, becomes important, and building interdependence in relationships becomes a high priority. Strong alliances, partnerships, and support systems are strategic and necessary for mutual business growth.

Relationship building is a gift I am blessed to have. It has enabled me to build some strategic partnerships with other business professionals. One strategic partnership was particularly important, as it opened the door to a success that I could not have predicted.

One of my capital projects was to develop a breakthrough manufacturing solution to drive the cost of manufacturing down for a particular product. I had the best team of technical experts who thought outside the box to define a solution. We had a solid foundation to build upon. We had a very compelling business need, as well as a clear path, to boost total share return for our shareholders.

Over several months, driven by our success criteria, our team developed what we thought was a winning concept. We were excited. Our business leaders were thrilled at the possibilities - if we could make them come alive! That machine would be unlike anything we currently had installed at our manufacturing plants. It would mark the beginning of a new era of manufacturing efficiency. Reluctantly, we parked our festive feelings until there was a proof of concept. We then presented our design concept and goals to our incumbent packaging equipment vendor. We requested a proposal to design and fabricate our concept. After a series of reviews, it became clear that our current equipment vendor was incapable of meeting our needs. Time to go to the Rolodex!

I learned of another vendor in Spain who was known to fabricate world-class machines. However, before I could approach that vendor, I received a great deal of pushback from my technical team, which was discouraging. Their illogical response begged some answers. Turning up my listening ears, I understood that, over the years, we had asked that vendor for proposals to fabricate equipment for us on several occasions. That vendor always came through with ideas and concepts, but we never closed a deal. Then came the excuses, clothed as reasons, as to why we never closed a deal with that vendor. My deduction was that they must be an attractive option for us. Why else would we keep going back to them? I therefore decided to set up a meeting with the vendor to discuss possibilities of a proposal.

I contacted the US agent of that vendor, Joel, and shared that the purpose for my call was to introduce myself as the new Engineering Leader for that technology, to give them a high-level view of where that part of our business was going and to see whether they would be interested in making a proposal to help us with our packaging equipment needs. First, there was a sarcastic laugh at the other end of the phone, then a question.

"You are not seriously asking me for a proposal, are you?" Joel asked.

I was suddenly thrust into a situation for which I was not prepared. My simple answer was, "Yes. I am. But would you mind sharing why you're so surprised?" We talked for another hour while I was given a history lesson on the relationship - or lack of one - between our companies.

After the call, my manager asked me how it went, to which I replied, "Bad! We have overdrawn their emotional bank account. Now I understand why God led me to this project. It's to leverage the ability He has blessed me with to build relationships." She smiled and nodded her head in agreement.

For the next two months, I held strategic discussions with that company. Each conversation became less adversarial. At one point, Joel shared a sales video with me that demonstrated the high-level technology they had. Their concepts and approach were exactly what we had envisioned. In parallel, my team was making solid progress against designing equipment in-house that would meet all our needs but with a timeline that was longer than desired.

Discussions with the new vendor progressed to the point where they were willing to entertain my request. I led a technical discussion session via video with them to share our needs and answer their 101 questions. Not long after, they were ready to present their proposal.

As a show of good faith, they invited me to their headquarters in Madrid, Spain, for the presentation of their proposal. As an act of replicating their good faith, I informed them that I would bring my manager and technical lead team to demonstrate this was more than just an empty request but a desire for a strategic partnership.

Ahead of the face-to-face meeting, my Vice President connected me with an internal Communications Specialist who specialized in strategic negotiations. She helped me plan and prepare for the event. She was God-sent! I did not even know this specific skill resided in-house as a discipline. Her coaching was invaluable and key to our success in building that partnership. I followed up on every one of her advices for preparation, including taking along various company products for a show-and-tell.

The meeting could not have gone better! After formal introductions, their CEO, who had flown into town for the meeting, kicked it off with his opening comments.

"Welcome, each one of you, to our company headquarters. Kennedy, I must say I appreciate what you have created with Joel and the team, which looks to me more like the partnership I would expect from your great company than a take-and-go vending machine approach. And thank you for giving us the chance to show you what we can do with our superb technology. Of course, I hope this blossoms into a great relationship, resulting in sales and you benefiting from our world-class machines." The CEO continued by sharing how much he admired our company and that he expected this to be the beginning of a much broader business model in which other business units in our company could benefit from their innovation.

My manager and I took over by introducing our business situation, which led to us talking about our need for new flexible technologies and why we believed this strategic partnership would be in both our interests. Our orchestrated presentation did its job to drive the business justification, communicate that our leadership was different, and convey our desire for a strategic partnership. They then shared a summary of their proposal, which covered all of our success criteria. A more detailed deep dive into the proposal would come after lunch. We were impressed with how easily they had converted our needs into a proposal.

I suddenly was not hungry. My corporate-America-work-through-lunch behavior surfaced when I asked about bringing lunch in. It was counteracted with their European, take-time-to-enjoy-your-meal perspective. So, we headed to the cafeteria.

A tour was scheduled after lunch before diving into the nuts and bolts of their proposal. Although I wanted to dive into the proposal first, I saw the tour as an opportunity to satisfy my desire to understand better and build my question list concerning their true capabilities.

After we put on our personal protective equipment of safety glasses, hard hats, and lab coats, there was an announcement. Joel faced us with this huge Cheshire cat grin on his face and said, "There is a surprise we would like to unveil on this tour. It is our latest innovation, and we believe you will be impressed by it. Now, we know how serious you are, and we want to show it to you. It is our proposal in real life!"

I kept trying to understand what Joel meant by "proposal in real life," until we rounded a corner to enter a large equipment production space and voila! It was a packaging equipment line under fabrication. According to Luis, their lead engineer, this would meet ninety percent of our success criteria with a completion schedule that accelerated our planned capital project's timeline by two years. I could feel my jaw hit the floor and my eyebrows hit the ceiling.

Taking the time to build that relationship paid me back in boatloads of dividends. I am reminded that you never know what will happen when you build a relationship with someone. That very person could just be the breakthrough you need.

"Keep on loving one another as brothers and sisters. Do not forget to show hospitality to strangers, for by so doing some people have shown hospitality to angels without knowing it." Hebrews 13:1–2 (NIV)

God's Grace

My company hires the smartest and brightest. However, there are some things engineering school does not teach: some doors need more than calculus or thermodynamics to open. By God's Grace, I am blessed with a skill and heart for relationships. I believe this contributed in large part to Joel opening up to me in our discussions, regardless of our company's history or how he personally felt.

My project was accelerated by more than two years - and it was not because of my intelligence. It was because, again, God's Grace led me to a company that was already working on a technology that met our needs.

Leadership Principles

1. Invest in the development of relationships.
2. Step out of your comfort zone if you want to get new and different results.
3. Collaboration accelerates results.

Chapter 2

Care for Others

Power Scripture:

This is how we've come to understand and experience love: Christ sacrificed his life for us. This is why we ought to live sacrificially for our fellow believers, and not just out for ourselves. If you see some brother or sister in need and have the means to do something about it but turn a cold shoulder and do nothing, what happens to God's love? It disappears. And you made it disappear.

1 John 3:16–17 (MSG)

Care for Others

Now, here is a leadership skill that I don't recall ever being a topic in any leadership training that I attended. As a leader, you must show you care for others by your words and your actions. Great leaders demonstrate all-around care. First, you show that you care upwards to your leaders as they support you. Secondly, you care sideways to your peers as they provide you with information. As we have read in the scriptures, *"iron sharpens iron," (Proverbs 27:17 [AMP]).* You must also show you care downwards to your subordinates if you want to empower them to deliver breakthrough results. Finally—and this one separates the self-confident leaders from the others—you must show you care outwardly to your critics. You don't have to greet them with a hug and a kiss, but you can be professional, humane, and concerned about their wellbeing. This act alone may keep your blood pressure down when you see them!

Caring does not mean giving in to every request. It does not mean you are *soft.* Caring for others does not mean you allow others to walk all over you. Sometimes, caring is demonstrated by "tough love." Other times, it requires you to take a firm stand to defend a position. It can sometimes take a strong dose of self-confidence and courageous leadership to demonstrate that you care for others.

You must show you care by treating all your employees fairly and valuing them. You demonstrate this by listening, showing empathy, and valuing their contributions. In some instances, you demonstrate you care by demanding they be treated fairly. Remember, although you may think your employees are shining stars, they are swimming in a tank with sharks . . . and those sharks do not care if your employees are cute or handsome!

You have to expect and be able to demand respect and fair treatment for your employees from sharks. If you don't care, the impact could be devastating to your effectiveness. However, if you do care, this is non-negotiable. That was my situation, as captured below.

I loved my job. I enjoyed leading a team to deliver uncommon results. My teams worked hard. Our results were built on excellence. One of my managers had a favorite saying: "Freedom comes with excellence." And that's what we pursued. The best part was annually showcasing the results of my team to our organization's staffing team. This administrative work was important, as it impacted their pay and progression. As a manager of others, my job was to put a high value on this effort. After all, it had the ability to affect each person's own livelihood. That's why I could not be quiet about another leader devaluing the great work of women in our organization.

I was always fully prepared for this meeting where we were going to review the contributions of our employees. Our collective, aligned assessment of each employee in our organization would go to our manager for final approval.

One summer, our manager made use of one of our company's benefits: an extended leave of absence. One of my peers was his backup for the position. This individual, Dave, was the most tenured among our leadership group and was the most lauded by our senior leaders, mostly because he knew how to *play the game*. However, he was a menacing ringleader of an all-white clique of my peers. Anthony was another one of my peers. He and I were the only African Americans at that level in our organization. We did not fit in. Although Anthony and I felt we were not welcomed, we were treated professionally by most of the other managers. Dave and his

17

clique of three others were not so discrete in their behavior toward us. They said Anthony was too militant. They thought I was too arrogant, and they did not know what to do with me. Being from the Caribbean and growing up in a different culture, I did not fit any of their molds or respond as they expected.

Our staffing assessment session was scheduled during the time our manager was out. Dave was the leader of the session. As you can imagine, the dynamics in this staff assessment meeting were less than culturally healthy. It did not help that I disliked and intentionally refused to get into the office politics. I did not play the game very well at all, and at that time, I was still naïve about the rules of the game. What did help was praying before these meetings. I would pray and recite Psalm 91, which talks about God taking care of me. I felt comforted, and my confidence increased after reciting even a part of that scripture.

The meeting was contentious, with the gang of four supporting one another's positions. It became obvious they had aligned on their positions before the meeting. A concept I learned in my Tae Kwon Do training was to never telegraph your next move. This means: do not let your opponent see which kick or punch you are about to execute or else they will easily evade, block, and counterattack. I was good at it and was therefore able to keep Dave and the others confused about my intentions by the leading questions I would ask. In addition, I loved to debate and became energized whenever I was told a flat out "no" to a request.

We started debating about one of my employees, Marcela. Marcela was using one of our company's other benefits: a reduced work schedule. Her results, which had been applauded by Dave in the past, all of a sudden became of little value. Confronting Dave head on would only serve to increase my stress level. He was in an egocentric zone, so I chose to capitalize on it to pull out what I already knew.

"Dave, do you think the reduced work schedule program has a bias to lower contributions?"

"Yes, it has, and that is okay if the women choose to use it," Dave replied.

"Great. I'm a little lost on this and need your help to ensure we assess the contributions correctly. So, you are saying, anyone on a reduced work schedule will, by definition, be doing less and therefore contributing less. Right?"

"Absolutely! It's not that they want to do less. They just do not have the time to get more done," Dave said, smiling confidently. The others added their agreements. Anthony was also in the meeting to present his employees' contributions. He wore his emotions on his sleeve, and I could read his facial expressions. He was about to explode!

"Thanks for that explanation, Dave. Now, you have heaped lots of praises on Marcela for her work this past year, describing her work as great. Was any of that a lie?" I asked jokingly. But I was not joking.

"No. It was my way of encouraging her. But I was not comparing it to others," he answered.

"Was this just because it's Marcela? Or do you see this applying to others on reduced work schedules?" I further asked. My face was serious now.

"It applies to all those on reduced work schedules," Dave responded.

"Dave, you realize our engineering department currently has three people on reduced work schedules, and they are all women who made a choice to spend more time at home. Right?"

"Yes, and I cannot see how a woman who is working a reduced work week of four days (versus five) could do more than a man who is working a full work week." Then he added the pièce de résistance . . . "That's why I seldom have women lead large projects."

At that point, I stood up, placed both palms on the conference table and in a firm but professional way shared my disapproval for his inaccurate opinion of a great employee benefit, his sexist position towards women, his confusion over the difference between activities and achievements, and (for added measure) for questioning my integrity. The fact is that Marcela, who was indeed on the reduced work week, was more efficient and diligent in her work. While her peers were busy with a myriad of activities and meetings, she would be busy making meaningful and impactful contributions to the business. She had a full work plan and was extremely creative in how she got her work done. Not only was she more productive, but her results were greater in value and consistency.

By the time I was finished addressing Dave's statements, all three men were patronizing me.

"You may not care about your employees," I stated, "but I certainly do care about mine and that you don't short-change any of them. I request that you reschedule this meeting and suggest that you three take time to reflect on your positions." I politely walked out of the meeting and straight to my human resource (HR) manager. I realized that I had never gotten angry, I'd just felt sad for Dave's ignorance and was amazed at his audacity. I knew that our manager had remained in communication with Dave. Therefore, I sent him and our HR leader an email, copying Dave for transparency, with a recount of the events and my assessment of my employees.

Because I had one of the larger groups of employees, the process could not be finalized without my input. A couple weeks later, and following some very tense meetings in which HR was involved, we finalized the assessment to my satisfaction. My direct report was assessed properly.

I updated my email signature with a principle I learned a few years before: *"People Need to know that you care, before they care what you know."* What I did not know then was that this principle would become a personal foundational principle throughout the rest of my corporate career.

God's Grace

I thank God for the courage He gave me to stand up to injustice and the control of my emotions in the fire. Although I had felt alone, I'd had faith that *"the One who is in you is greater than the one who is in the world" 1 John 4:4 (NIV)*. God was on my side, and this gave me the courage to demonstrate how much I cared for my employees. They worked hard and deserved a leader who also worked hard for them. Upon his return, my manager asked me to lead a couple diversity training sessions for our leadership team.

Leadership Principles

1. Courageous leaders stand up to injustice.
2. Never confuse activity with achievement.
3. People need to know that you care before they care what you know.

Chapter 3

Become An Advocate

Sponsorship

As a leader, you should look for and support good talent by using your power and influence to advance others' aspirations. When you are committed to providing someone with advancement support in their career or area of interest, that is sponsorship. In business, a sponsor is an upper-level manager who can directly impact career growth in areas like more challenging assignments and even advancement. This person makes things happen. As a leader with hierarchical influence and responsibilities, you are in a great position to fill that role.

Sponsors are personally vested in the progression and professional development of their protégés. They stand up for and present their individuals as capable candidates for developmental positions and/or promotions. This means these advocates must have a working knowledge of their protégés' skills and accomplishments. They must also be directly involved or have the ability to influence the supporting formal systems like promotion and assignment planning. Sponsors should also have access to other influential people and key career growth opportunities. Sponsorship is an important part of the development system for top managers. It can be considered as an integral part of succession planning.

There are times when the person you sponsor may not even be aware of your advocacy or of how you are supporting them in the background. There are other times when the relationship is more overt. In my case, I got to experience a master supporter at work, inspiring me to be an effective leader like her.

God blessed me with a great sponsor, Brenda. She was actively committed to my development and success. She had proven, on several occasions, that she had my best interests at heart. It was not because I was smart but because she believed that ensuring I was treated fairly was the right thing to do. Brenda knew my skills and capabilities. Looking back over the few short years from our original meeting, I realized she always encouraged me into deeper waters to take up more challenging assignments. Often, she would have a hand in certain career doors being opened for me. Such was the case when a job opening that I was qualified for came up in her organization, which was also a promotion opportunity for me. Of course, the best proof of a sponsor's commitment is to offer you a job in their organization if you are the best candidate.

I learned through a round-about way of Brenda's job opening. That same day, I decided to connect with her to ask if she was still accepting applicants and share my desire to apply. That particular job was different from the assignments I'd had since being introduced to Brenda several years back. Therefore, she was less familiar with the skills I had acquired that would enable my success in that job. But I assumed she knew my background enough to know I could do well if selected. Because I did not have a scheduled appointment with her, I did a quick drop-in at her desk.

"Brenda, I understand there is an opportunity for a senior-level manager in your organization. I just wanted you to know I'll be applying for it."

Brenda expressed both excitement and surprise that I would be applying. "I am glad you want to apply. And you should know that I would absolutely love to have you in a job that reports directly to me. However, it is not an engineering role, which is what you are used to. It is actually in business administration. I knew you had a stint in that area in the past, but do you think you would be able to compete with my other candidates?" Brenda asked.

"I believe so," I replied. "And in fact, I already have ideas and a vision of making this job even more productive."

"OK. I'll tell you what. Go ahead and apply. My administrative assistant will set up the interview. I will be looking forward to that. Be ready to share with me what you think I need to know about you that I don't already know. I have always been impressed with your results, so I'm excited to learn more." She was all smiles.

Before applying, I prayed to God and asked that if this was His will for my career that nothing would stand in my way. I also prayed that if this was not His will that He would allow me to learn from the experience and be at peace in my heart with the outcome.

I applied. The interview was scheduled. I was nervous - but not about my skills or the fact that I felt like I was reaching for the stars. I was nervous that I would disappoint my sponsor.

At the interview, Brenda started, "This job requires a lot of time in developing countries. I know you were born in Dominica. So, my first question is: What other experiences do you have with working in developing countries and understanding their cultures?"

I smiled. "Well, I can tell you a lot about my work in developing countries in Latin America and Asia, particularly, but let me start by sharing that I was not only born in Dominica, but that's where I also grew up. I came to the US as an adult."

Brenda's eyes widened. "Oh, how cool! We need to talk about that sometime! I was not aware of that tidbit of info! I thought you grew up in the South! OK. Here is my second question: Aside from the job you did three years ago in my business, what other experiences do you have in the business administration function?"

"I actually led a corporate global Business Administration team, which was made up of members from each of our corporate business units, for three years. During that time, I went around the world training teams on that particular work process. Not only am I certified and have worked in that work process, but I am also an instructor. I have held more than fifteen training sessions across Asia, Latin America, Europe, and the US. "

"Okay. Freeze. I need more paper to take better notes." Brenda could hardly contain her excitement as she flew out of her chair and made a mad dash out of the conference room to grab a pen and notepad.

This was encouraging. But it was painfully obvious to me that I had not done a good enough job of empowering my sponsor. I had not equipped her with enough detailed information about me to fully prepare her to be my advocate. If she was not the master of a sponsor that she was, I most likely would not have been given this opportunity to share my capabilities.

Thank God I was awarded the job, and Brenda proved to be an even better manager and inspirational leader than I had imagined her to be. Brenda was undoubtedly the best sponsor that I knew. I now had firsthand experience of her advocacy on my behalf. This lasting experience was very eye-opening for me. It was full of lessons I could learn from. However, although Brenda had represented me well, I had not initially taken the time I needed to take her through my history with sufficient depth. What I now recommend and know would have been more impactful is compiling a short video or podcast of my background and skills and forwarding it ahead of an interview. A bulleted one-pager biographical data sheet was not adequate. I attributed that to me not wanting to waste her time. In fact, I remember her chastising me with those piercing eyes and motherly smile. "You know, I can manage my time better than you can manage it for me. So, if you need me, just get on my calendar and no excuses! If you can't get on my calendar for an urgent need, send me a text, email, or phone message, and I'll move some things around."

I was impressed with her approach of giving me the opportunity to share with her what I wanted her to know about me rather than assuming that she already knew me. Had she gone with that assumption, it would have denied me this golden opportunity and denied her the best candidate.

Brenda not only gave me a promotion, but she also taught me valuable lessons about being an effective sponsor. This strengthened my toolbox to be an even greater leader.

God's Grace

I do not believe I learned of Brenda's role by accident. I do not believe Brenda was being charitable to interview me. I believe God had prepared me for this job long ago. He opened up my understanding of the job and blessed me with an open-minded sponsor who opened the door for me to step into my future.

"Let each of you esteem and look upon and be concerned for not merely his own interests, but also, each of the interests of others." Philippians 2:4 (AMP)

God is the best example of a sponsor. He is my active advocate and is truly committed to my development and advancement to eternal salvation.

Leadership Principles

1. Reach back to pull someone with you as you climb the ladder of success.
2. Be authentic. It avoids a lot more pain than it creates.
3. Allow your protégés to update you on what they think you already know about them.

Chapter 4

Create Harmony

Power Scripture:

I have a serious concern to bring up with you, my friends, using the authority of Jesus, our Master. I'll put it as urgently as I can: you must get along with each other. You must learn to be considerate of one another, cultivating a life in common.

1 Corinthians 1:10 (MSG)

Collaboration

Collaboration is when two or more parties - people, teams, organizations, or companies - join forces to work on something of mutual interest in order to deliver a particular objective or goal. In some cases, the outcome is only achievable by working together. In other cases, the outcome will deliver better results through the partnership.

Collaboration is about sharing information, knowledge, talents, or capital to meet the objective. The expectation is that the outcome will be more beneficial. This could mean an acceleration of results, a more robust outcome, or even a higher quality outcome. It is a strategic partnership for the parties involved, whether individuals or companies.

Collaboration cannot be assumed to be achievable simply because two parties identify a common objective and sign an agreement to work together. Collaboration is tough work when two different organizations try to work together. Differences in culture, structure, approach, and even language could be significant barriers to success. Underestimating the work required to build the foundation of a collaborative agreement could be detrimental to its success. A non-collaborative team is like a horse stuck in the mud - a lot of horsepower but going nowhere fast. Typically, team members make constant emotional withdrawals from each other, leaving dismal results and non-existent accountability. However, when collaboration is done right, the results can be quite satisfying.

It is important that leaders foster a culture of collaboration in their organizations. The outcome will be the delivery of breakthrough results. However, it all starts with the leader demonstrating good collaboration skills. God opened a door for me to help one team move from combative to collaborative, and they watched as results surfaced.

In my team, the technical resources, which supported the African business, were not collaborative. They were operating in a dysfunctional environment, with everyone taking credit for results but no one taking ownership for problems. This was the result of the engagement of two different businesses trying to work together, with the leaders not taking the time to do the foundational work of building a spirit of teamwork.

The work was stressful. The technical director, who was from the other business, said he was building the team to be agile and to maneuver like a fighter jet. Unfortunately, he was really building a culture of fly-by-the-seat-of-your-pants. There were very few systems designed to support this new organization, so all involved defaulted to their previous experiences, which were, in many cases, in conflict with each other. Everyone had good intentions, but the execution was painful. When successful, it was great. However, the failures were organizationally bloody, with many dead bodies in the wake. Having a competitive spirit did not help reduce the stress. Increased stress meant heightened emotions. Team culture suffered.

That technical team was made up of primarily three key functions: technology development, quality assurance, and manufacturing. One of the functional leaders, Alexandre, recognized the serious organizational issues and requested that the whole team get together to discuss the problem. Alexandre had a dominant, "Type A" personality. His style was very passionate and agile. From his perspective, systems were meant to be "loose" guides and were not meant to be followed as designed. There was no shortage of confidence in him, and he was very happy to tell you his thoughts. One of the other functional leaders, Clive, was the polar opposite. His work (and style) was centered around laws and regulations, and he operated by standards, work plans, and templates. He was less vocal but, being technically sharp, would debate with facts and figures. His strategy annoyed Alexandre, who declared that Clive was not thinking and that the world was not black-and-white. Clive agreed to get together but had a different idea for a moderator than Alexandre. Alexandre then recommended they use me as someone they could all align with because I was a strong collaborator. Plus, I already had a positive working relationship with all their teams. Clive and the other leader, Deborah, agreed. I attribute my ability to work with others to the spirit of God in me. I always keep in front of me the power scripture of this chapter.

After my first conference call with Clive, Deborah, and Alexandre, it became clear that my work had to start with them. As expected, they each had what they thought was the best idea on how to address the current culture. After I allowed each of them to plead their case, I shared my premise that the culture of a team is a reflection of the leader. I also shared my thoughts on what was needed for them to get on the same sheet of music. They were all excited. That was a good sign, because not only did they *need* help, but they truly *wanted* help.

I designed a three-phased approach. Phase one was me working with the three leaders. We had a thoughtful first event. At the conclusion, I asked each one to share one affirmation with the others. Following that session, I received individual phone calls from Deborah and Alexandre and had a meeting with Clive. Each one expressed how impactful the affirmations were to them and how excited they were about the main event. Alexandre shared that he had no idea Deborah had anything positive to say about him because they were always fighting. He was touched, and he really wanted his team to experience a collaborative culture. That was further confirmation that the leaders really wanted to drive change.

Phase two was getting a sense of the organization internally from the perspectives of all their bosses, whom I had already connected with and enrolled in the process. I needed management to recognize and reward the right behaviors.

Phase three was a global summit with all three teams together in the same city. We chose Paris as an ideal location for the team members, who were coming from Africa, Europe, and the US. We worked through a very difficult schedule and were able to squeeze in the event between other commitments and the Christmas break.

I designed and facilitated a two-day summit that leveraged the diversity the team brought from different cultures, backgrounds, and work experiences. Among the topics, we discussed communication styles, cultural biases, work approaches, and expectations within various levels in the organization. I used simple tools to help the members do some self-searching and understand the strengths of others. At the start of the summit, I partnered each member with another individual, preferably one with whom they had not worked closely. In that partnership, both parties would be accountable to one another during and post the summit.

As I had hoped, the partners started building bonds that strengthened their relationships, and the grassroots change began as they learned more and more about and cared for each other. It started with each person wanting to be the best partnership - partners getting creative and giving gifts to others. The change started. Ending discussions during breaks, like lunch and coffee breaks, became increasingly difficult, as the partners had no shortage of things to laugh and talk about. Language was no barrier. The competition became friendly, with everyone cheering each other on through challenges I posed.

The trio of leaders accepted the call to duty and demonstrated the desired results. We ended the summit by actually applying their new learnings to one of the most challenging projects they were working on. Less than five minutes into the exercise, the team erupted in laughter. They realized that a simple concept was totally misunderstood and had driven months of frustration among two of the teams. There was clarity about some of the bottlenecks, an understanding of legal boundaries, and a working and aligned action plan was developed. What they had been trying to do for months had gotten done in one afternoon!

The whole team commented on the information gained and gave their thoughts on the execution of the summit. Alexandre openly shared at the closing of the event that so much pain would have been avoided in the technical team if they had only taken the time to be more collaborative. No kidding! As the Good Book says, *"How good and pleasant it is when God's people live together in unity!"* *Psalms 133:1 (NIV).*

The three leaders committed to demonstrate and foster a more collaborative culture. Although I was exhausted from the event - and still jetlagged - it felt good to see how God could shine through me. However, there was one more agenda item: affirmations. I gave each member a notepad and asked each to write words of affirmations to each of the other members. I then asked them to place the affirmations in a gift journal I handed to each member as a reminder of the summit. They could all then take the notes back as gifts. It was magical!

God's Grace

Reflecting on the event and its success, I could see the Hand of God in the process. First, months before I'd received the request for help, I had been exposed to a concept that really resonated with me. I took the time to understand the concept in detail and grew a desire to teach it. As it is said, the best way to learn is to teach. Little did I know that God was preparing me for the Paris summit. That new concept formed the basis for the training I developed for our technical team.

Second, I made a request for office supply materials to be ready and available at the meeting for the participants. Based on my experience, I decided, if possible, that I would purchase a few more items - just as back-up - upon arrival to my hotel. Having the right materials was instrumental to the success of the group exercises. I arrived late to my hotel on Sunday evening. However, I was blessed to find a fully stocked office supply store right next to my hotel. The store manager was willing to stay open long enough (on a Sunday night) to allow me to make my purchases. The next morning, I learned that the administrative assistant had not completed my request for materials. This was a casualty of the adversarial culture that had existed. The supplies I purchased were all I had available. But it was enough.

God favored me by opening a door for me to lead this event, preparing me with the needed information and supplies, and helping me execute a riveting event that was a success in driving collaboration amongst a team that had been struggling for some time.

Leadership Principles

1. The culture of an organization is a reflection of the leader.
2. Workers want to do the right thing. They just need guidance.
3. Collaboration drives breakthrough results.

Chapter 5

Your Word is Gold

Power Scripture:

Above all, my brothers and sisters, do not swear - not by heaven or by earth or by anything else. All you need to say is a simple "Yes" or "No." Otherwise you will be condemned.

James 5:12 (NIV)

Integrity

I believe an organization is a reflection of its leader, which is then reflected in the culture of the organization. That culture is driven by what the leader says, does, and demonstrates. The words, actions, and behavior of a leader matter. If a leader is dishonest, untrustworthy, and lacks authenticity, that leader will foster a culture lacking integrity.

Integrity is being true to your word. It is abiding by the agreement of a handshake. As a leader, integrity matters. Integrity is the constant and unwavering demonstration of ethical values and principles and high moral standards. This is easier to do when you are under a microscope and being held accountable by others. It is more difficult when you have to hold yourself accountable to do what is right when no one is looking or there to keep you honest. That is why integrity in the business world is a gauge of your truthfulness. Situations will come to an end, but your integrity and character will outlast you.

A leader who acts with integrity will do what is right for the customers, employees, and business. Integrity is one of the most important basic characteristics of a leader. It is exponentially more meaningful when leaders can hold themselves accountable when no one is watching. What shows strong integrity is when you, as a leader, do not even have to question whether or not you should compromise your moral or ethical standards. It is non-negotiable, as was demonstrated in my situation.

I have traveled to China for business and pleasure multiple times. I love the Chinese people and their culture. I have developed many close relationships over the years with them and have also learned a lot about business etiquette and norms in China. This started with my first visit to the land of the panda bear.

I went to China to negotiate a deal with a company to manufacture a product for my company. That company had technical and organizational capability that was superior to their competition, whom we were considering. Their security process and approach to managing the counterfeit risk was especially attractive. My options analysis gave them the advantage and pointed directionally to a lower risk for us by partnering with them.

Bai Zhao, my Chinese sponsor and colleague, personally knew the company from a previous job he'd held in the Chinese government. He validated the information and data that the company had shared with us. This was a model company that any Western corporation would want to partner with. This was during the period when Western businesses were looking more and more to Chinese suppliers for lower manufacturing costs, as well as to expand their footprint into Asia. Therefore, I pushed for us to get a contract quickly to solidify the capacity. Bai Zhao was not in a hurry and expressed a desire to negotiate some more.

A little anxious, I said, "Bai, we need to move faster! Don't you know *the early bird catches the first worm?*"

"That may be in the West," he replied, laughing. "In China, we say, 'The early deer gets shot by the hunter!'" And my appreciation for the diversity of cultures increased.

We got to a point where the negotiation was at a stalemate. I made a bold recommendation to my manager for me to visit the supplier to perform a detailed manufacturing capability assessment before deciding whether to accept their final offer. The supplier accepted my request to visit their plant, which was located in Weifang, China. Bai proudly shared that Weifang was the birthplace of the kite and is the kite capital of the world.

That was a critical trip. Therefore, I paid a little more attention to the details of the trip and the meetings we would have. The assessment would follow our standard capability assessment process for contract manufacturers. I was joined by colleagues from other functions (quality, safety, and purchases) from our Shanghai plant.

I arranged to arrive on Saturday night from the US so that I could take Sunday to recuperate. Most importantly, I wanted to give myself time to do some shopping if my luggage did not make it on my flight, as had been the case on my very first trip to Beijing. Of course, you do not want to walk into such a critical meeting looking like you just rolled out of bed, do you? Me neither.

I received a call from Bai on Sunday morning.

"Good morning, Mr. Kennedy," Bai began. "How was your sleep?"

"It was five-star great considering this is a five-star hotel," I joked.

"Did you enjoy a good Chinese breakfast this morning?" I could almost hear Bai smiling on the other end of the phone.

"I did! It was made up of pancakes, orange juice, and scrambled eggs!" I laughed.

"It's OK. You will get real Chinese food tonight. Mr. Liu, the plant owner, is inviting you to dinner tonight with him and his leadership team. He said it will be a light dinner, nothing formal, but he was impressed with your preparation and approach to the meeting and wanted to meet with you before the work started on Monday." At least, that was the story shared with Bai.

I accepted and thought nothing of it. In fact, I welcomed the help to stay awake, as jet lag usually hits me the hardest around dinnertime.

It was clear, upon arrival to the restaurant, that their definition of a "light dinner" was different from mine. We occupied the entire top floor of what appeared to be an elite club. Mr. Liu and his leadership team were already there, and the atmosphere was festive, although no one was eating or drinking. Everyone was just talking and laughing over the music. Bai explained that they had been waiting for me to arrive. I could tell that dinner was going to be the customary family style with a never-ending parade of dishes presented by beautifully adorned, smiling, graceful, and polite servers.

The seating had been prearranged. I was seated next to the owner at the head of the table. Bai was seated next to me. A host offered me a glass and was about to pour in the alcohol. At that split second, I remembered a small detail of my well-crafted plan that had been missed. I knew the importance that was typically placed on drinking alcohol, so I was to inform the owner that I did not drink alcohol. I kicked myself, then tried to politely and discreetly pass on the alcohol. Mr. Liu held up his hand, and the noisy room suddenly quieted.

Bai turned to me and said, "You must drink with him! It is not okay not to accept!"

I said, "Sorry, Bai, but I do not drink alcohol. I am so sorry I forgot to share that with you and him."

There was a flurry of Chinese exchange followed by laughter and, with a wave of his hand, Mr. Liu said, "Beer OK!"

My sponsor turned to me grinning and said, "Mister Liu said it is okay. You can have a beer."

I smiled sheepishly and felt my embarrassment and my cheeks turning red under my melanin complexion even before I responded. "Beer is also alcohol. No thank you."

He then replied, "Oh no. No alcohol. Only beer. Beer, no alcohol."

I realized I had to be clearer. "Due to my religious beliefs, I do not drink alcohol and will not be drinking tonight. And in my culture, beer is considered alcohol." So, I accepted ginger ale.

Based on my knowledge of the cultural norms, I knew I had created an uphill battle for negotiations the next day, so I decided I would enjoy the dinner and re-strategize when I got back to the hotel. I enjoyed the rest of the evening as we exchanged jokes and I answered ninety-nine questions about America and the West from the team. They enjoyed their time with me, and I enjoyed my time with them.

On the way back to the hotel, I asked Bai Zhao how deep of a hole I had created. He laughed and explained how happy they were to meet me and how surprised and pleased they were with my open interaction with them, although I was the "boss." He said that one of the employees said that I made them feel important. Back in my hotel room, I prayed and remembered one particular scripture: *"Stand up for Me among the people you meet and The Son of Man will stand up for you before all God's Angels" Luke 12:8 (MSG).* I definitely needed that assurance.

The next morning, Bai met me for breakfast and a quick review before his driver took us to the plant. When we got to the meeting room, we were both handed a folder for the meeting. I asked where to set up my computer for my presentation so that I could be ready following the welcomes and introductions. I needed to try to undo the damage I must have done to the trust level the prior evening.

Right at that time, Mr. Liu walked in, shook my hand, and having heard my request, said, "No need to set up computer." He then let out a string of Chinese to Bai. Everyone was smiling politely. It was beautiful but hard to read between the lines. I was trying to smile but was more focused on the knot in my tummy.

Mr. Liu turned to me and proceeded in English, "There is a saying: 'If you can trust me to get drunk with me, I can trust you to do business with you.' But last night, you showed me something else: integrity. You did not compromise your religious beliefs, even 7,000 miles from home. This means your words and your name are strong." He emphasized the word "strong" while clenching his fists and pumping them upwards to chest level. "This means I can trust you to do business. In the folder is my signed agreement accepting your latest offer. We can continue with the rest of the program, but I want to do business with someone who has high integrity and who makes my employees feel important. And you did that last night, and I could see it was real."

Whew! I exhaled internally. I did not need to read between those lines. He was very clear, and my smile was very real! I rewarded myself by going to the silk market that evening. There, I was reminded, again, that they love to negotiate . . . I mean haggle!

What distinguishes top leaders? . . . *"One is uncompromising integrity. I mean that in a moral sense, but I also mean it in the sense of thinking integrity and action integrity. They think with discipline and honesty. They sort through flattery, through politics, and seeing things as they are, come to grips with reality, and then bring incredible integrity to the decision and the action." –A.G. Lafley, Former P&G CEO*

God's Grace

They seem like simple concepts: Treat others like you want to be treated. Everyone is important. Stand firm with integrity, and do not compromise your values. God used these simple principles to open doors and give me favor in one night that months of negotiation had not done.

Leadership Principles

1. The words and actions of a leader matter.
2. Take time to learn and value the diversity around you.
3. Have a high standard of integrity, and do not compromise your values.

Chapter 6

Sharing Wisdom

Power Scripture:

So I exhort the elders among you, as a fellow elder and a witness of the sufferings of Christ, as well as a partaker in the glory that is going to be revealed: shepherd the flock of God that is among you, exercising oversight, not under compulsion, but willingly, as God would have you; not for shameful gain, but eagerly; not domineering over those in your charge, but being examples to the flock. And when the chief Shepherd appears, you will receive the unfading crown of glory. Likewise, you who are younger, be subject to the elders. Clothe yourselves, all of you, with humility toward one another, for "God opposes the proud but gives grace to the humble."

1 Peter 5:1–5 (ESV)

Mentoring

No one can be successful by themselves. Those who think they are really are not giving credit to those who have supported them. Mentoring can improve the trajectory of a life or a career. Mentoring should be a key strategy of leaders to give back to others.

A mentor is a trusted and experienced advisor who acts as a sounding board for whatever their mentee has to share. The mentor provides their mentees insights and perspectives based on their experiences. This includes counseling, guidance, and offering advice about skill development and organization. Personal and professional discussions are the basis for a close, trusting relationship. Strong mentor-mentee relationships are very satisfying in that the leader sees the growth and development of a mentee and enjoys their positive impact, knowing he or she made a difference in someone's life or career.

Although physical distance can be a challenge, some of my strongest mentor-mentee relationships were international. These required some more effort on my part to make the engagements happen, but that resulted in more effective connections. When mentors do not put much effort into a relationship, the connections are inadequate. Unlike some mentors, I place a higher value on the relationship. If I do not hear from a mentee for a while, I will reach out to check in. Each check-in may be one of the times I am most needed to provide a listening ear. Some mentees also need guidance on how to foster and leverage the relationship as part of their development. We all have gotten to a place where it's hard to stop and seek help. So, it's important for the mentor to reach out to the mentee.

I am committed as a leader to be available to my mentees. If you choose this level of commitment, the results can be very gratifying, even in the very simple, no-energy-needed-on-your-part exchanges, as in my situation below.

One of my mentees, Anna, called me late one evening to discuss the status of her new assignment. She had been passed up for a promotion in her previous role and felt she had not been rewarded for the significant contributions she'd made to the company and her previous discipline, finance. This led to her moving to a new discipline for a fresh start.

It was great to see how Anna's new managers were demonstrating true appreciation for her skills. Not surprisingly, she started receiving numerous accolades after only three months in the new role. However, one day, she called me because she had a situation on her hands. A promotion had been announced two weeks prior for one of her peers in finance.

Everyone in her previous discipline seemed to be concerned about Anna's reaction to her peer's promotion. One of her previous managers asked her if she regretted moving. Another offered a listening ear if she wanted to talk. One of her new managers told her not to lose faith because they were working to fast-track a promotion for her in her new discipline.

Anna started feeling overwhelmed and just wanted to focus on her job. She said she was very appreciative of her new organization and loved her new manager. Now, she really wanted to onboard well and do a good job.

She said, "Kennedy, I cannot do both a good job here and be pushing for my promotion. I wish everyone would respect that and quit stressing me out. I feel appreciative for the second chance in this new team and just want to do a good job, considering they have been so good to me. Kennedy, is it too much that I told my sponsor that I cannot spend a lot of time thinking about promotion right now and that I just want to do a good job?"

I asked, "Is it okay if I ask you a few questions?"

"Yes," she replied.

"Has this company invested a lot in your growth and development?"

"Yes."

"Would you consider yourself one of P&G's most valuable assets?"

"Yes," she replied.

"If you have an asset, would you want to get the best return possible on your investment?"

"Absolutely!" she said with a confident laugh. "Who wouldn't?"

"Well," I said, "what about if the asset wanted to just relax for a while and did not want to be used to its full potential? Would you feel that asset is doing the right thing? As you know," I continued, "you are classified as 'ready to be promoted,' which means you are already demonstrating the skills and behaviors needed to be successful at the next level. This means you are currently being sub-optimized and the company is not benefiting from your full potential."

Anna thought for a while and, while deep in thought, said slowly, "Hmmmm. You are right." Then, with an accelerating tone of voice, she continued, "Although finance did not value me enough to reward me, P&G has been great to me, but I can't do both. I guess I shall push for my promotion because I know sooner or later my current responsibilities will not be enough for me." Then, as if a light bulb had gone on, she declared, "I need to change my focus. Right?" She was now seeking confirmation.

"Wrong," I answered. I could sense her deflation through the phone. I continued, "You need to keep focusing on doing an outstanding job where you are, and do not focus on pushing for a promotion. However, don't close any doors that God is opening to you. You have two objectives: doing a great job *and* being ready to step into the opportunity when it comes. Do not tell others that you don't want to focus on your promotion. They will take that to mean you are no longer interested. This carries a double-negative weight for you as both a woman and an African American. Instead, thank them for their support and sponsorship and let them know you will make sure you remain ready when the call comes. If you keep saying that you are not focused on being promoted right now, then the future will never come, and your words will hold you back. Others will not help because of the message you have unintentionally communicated. Instead, be strategic in your messaging."

I could sense the weight lifting. She was ecstatic and said, "Kennedy, you have no idea how you have truly changed my life over these past few years providing guidance and mentoring me."

"No. It's not me, my friend. God has been gracious to me through my experiences, and that has allowed me to share with others like you," I responded.

God's Grace

God has blessed me with wisdom developed through my experiences and given me a deep empathy, allowing me to listen, coach, guide, and help others see through their challenges. This unmerited favor has caused others to listen to me and has allowed me to pour into their lives. In turn, I am blessed to be a blessing.

Leadership Principles

1. Great leaders have a desire to unselfishly share from their vast experiences and develop others to become greater leaders.
2. Every great leader has a foundation of support through mentors, coaches, and sponsors.
3. Be willing to listen. You may just save a career, a future, or a life.

Chapter 7

A Listening Heart

Power Scripture:

*Rejoice with those who rejoice [sharing others' joy],
and weep with those who weep [sharing others' grief].*

Romans 12:15 (AMP)

Empathy

There are many leaders. What separates the greatest leaders from the rest is their demonstration of leadership from the heart. They have empathy. Empathy is the ability to be aware of and to understand a person's situation, including their feelings and thoughts. It is as close as you can get to walking in someone else's shoes and communicating that you see, hear, and feel their emotions. So, as a leader, you must develop good listening and sensing skills.

Empathetic leaders show their organizations that they care, resulting in a healthy environment with open communication. They are best able to help an employee navigate problems they face. These employees, in turn, can bring their *whole* self to work and thereby operate at their fullest.

You do not have to be a *touchy-feely* person to be empathetic. It is not about being sympathetic (feeling of concern) to someone's situation or loss. And it is different from compassion (empathetic understanding with a desire to help). You can develop and demonstrate empathy by learning to see another person's point of view and actively listen to them non-judgmentally while trying to understand their situation. It is about seeing from the other person's point of view. Empathy requires a caring heart and a desire to provide emotional support. Empathy requires authenticity. As a leader, demonstrating empathy to your employees communicates that you care and that they are important, like your most valuable asset.

I am blessed with a passion to help others avoid experiencing the challenges I faced as a minority in corporate America. However, I do not go out looking to help others. Those needing help seemingly gravitate towards me. I believe God places me where I can be used to help others. That is a path I value and always make time for. Sometimes, the one needing help is not an individual but an entire team.

After many years in P&G and a couple plant assignments, I had become a master in one particular skill area. Four years after moving back to the technical offices, I was asked to relocate again to another facility to help in that particular skill. The plan was to go in, do a quick assessment of the issues, implement plans to close the gaps, and establish a long-term continuity of the results. Once there, my strategy was to train, coach, and empower the leadership team so they would drive the cultural change we needed to get the desired results. I took my work to the shop floor among the site employees. Over a relatively short period of time, I noticed an imbalance. The site had a majority representation of women managers but somewhere south of ten percent representation on the leadership team.

As I met and got to know the female managers, I was struck by the stress they each carried, feeling unsupported, underrepresented, undervalued, and overworked. On the surface, they appeared to be thriving from their positive attitudes and perpetual smiles. However, behind the façade was the turbulent spirits of bodies carrying heavy weights they were not designed to carry, mixed with a cupful of pain and a pound of unappreciation. That mental concoction could disempower anyone.

One of the women on the team I inherited had been filling in as our team's temporary leader for almost a year. She was carrying more than her fair share of the load in our area and was not being recognized for her leadership skills or rewarded for her contributions. Another woman on my new team was delivering her work plan, but it was from her pure passion for environmental sustainability rather than being valued or empowered to do her job. These women were not well-represented at the table where decisions were being made. I found myself increasingly providing impromptu coaching to a few of them.

One day, I received a generic invitation to one of their regular Women Managers Network meetings. I accepted the invitation but asked one of the women on my team what the invitation was about so that I could be better prepared. All she told me was that zero preparation was needed, that they had a request for me, and that more would be shared at the meeting. She smiled and said, "It's nothing to worry about." But that did not satisfy my curiosity. I felt like I was being summoned to the principal's office. The agony of the wait was less than comforting.

I joined the meeting at the appointed time. They spent the first half checking in on each other's individual statuses. I was shocked at what I heard. I could not believe we had a team feeling so disempowered. It was painful to listen to the weight this talented group of managers was carrying.

The team had to put the rest of the team members' check-ins on hold so they could proceed with the rest of the agenda, which was a proposal for me. Before they could continue, I asked if it was okay for me to ask a few questions concerning what I had just witnessed. They gave me the green light. I asked a few probing questions to understand how they were taking the initiative to seek help for the issues they were experiencing. The response came down to "fear" after failed attempts to raise their voices and the consequences they experienced. One member, Krista, had already been mentally driven halfway out the door. She feared that one mistake would lead to her being asked to leave the company. She was not being valued, her style was not appreciated, and her cultural differences were being brushed aside.

What the Women Managers Network team confided in me was raw, excruciating pain. They had bloody knees from crawling their way to a professional success target that was always moving. Thirty minutes after the meeting was scheduled to end, we were still talking.

It was the end of the day on a Friday, and none of us had any more scheduled meetings that day, so we were in no rush to end.

At some point, I asked what requests they had for me. Karen, the team leader, pulled up a slide presentation. The title was "Proposal for a Kalamazoo Site WMN Team Sponsor." I did not need a presentation to guess what was being requested. The last ninety minutes had been more powerful than a slide deck. I turned to the leader and said, "Karen, you took time to prepare this presentation, and I appreciate it. Therefore, if you desire to go through it, I will listen. However, my answer is 'Yes.' I will sponsor this team."

Karen responded, "We already see you as our sponsor. The last hour and a half with us have been the most any manager has spent with us seeking to understand our situation. You have shown more care for us in your short time here than anyone else." Those words I personally will never forget because I had done nothing special since arriving at the site except be empathetic.

Before closing, I offered a few suggestions for the path moving forward, which included developing a charter for the team. I shared that I would formally communicate my sponsorship to my business leaders, so that I could bring more visibility to them and increase accountability on the site to support them. I also shared that I expected my communication would bring advocacy to them from leadership outside the facility. It would also send a message that this team was important and valued. I offered to lead a training session once a month to provide coaching on the team's individual leadership skills, as well as their collective network development. Finally, I requested a "getting to know you," one-on-one join-up with each team member over the following thirty days.

When I left the site a couple years later, representation on the leadership team had dramatically improved for the women managers. Several had been promoted, and the one who had been viewed as having performance issues was highly rated and had been appointed to a critical role. Our people are our most valuable *assets*. As leaders, we must stop, listen, and feel their joys and pains - and take appropriate action.

"If you take away our money, our buildings and our brands, but leave us our people, we can rebuild the whole thing in a decade . . ."
- Richard Deupree, Former P&G CEO

God's Grace

At my 25th service anniversary celebration, Krista attended and spoke. She shared with the group the impact that I'd had on her and the rest of the team at that site and that I was the reason she was still with the company, where she was highly regarded for her technical skills and had received multiple promotions. In reality, all I had done was what any good manager of others would do: care. It was God's favor on my life that allowed me to carry out my mission to be a blessing to others like Krista.

Leadership Principles

1. Stop. Sit. Listen to your employees.
2. Real leadership starts with the heart.
3. Be empathetic to those under your leadership.

Section II
Leading with Your Hands

Chapter 8

Excellence

Power Scripture:

*Poor is he who works with a negligent and idle hand,
But the hand of the diligent makes him rich.*

Proverbs 10:4 (AMP)

Diligence

As leaders, we have to make many decisions. Some are data-based, and the reality is, some are not. However, when we can, we should do the due diligence to get the right data to make the best decision for the business. As a leader, ask for the data. As W. Edwards Deming once said, *"In God we trust. All others must bring data."*

Diligence means taking the time needed to do the hard but necessary work persistently. It means to take care to do the job right the first time. Go the extra mile if necessary. Do it with purpose and determination. Do it with excellence.

It is a leader's job to ensure a task is done with diligence by probing for data. If you are not a diligent leader, it is very likely you will allow mediocrity and accept the results of poorly penetrated problems. You must ensure your foundation is not being built on a sand dune. Sometimes, we have to do the due diligence and go after the data ourselves.

God gave me favor in the situation below, in which resources from multiple organizations rallied behind me to develop the data needed to help make the right decision for the company.

My business unit was in a collaborative initiative with another business. As a key representative from my business unit, I raised the flag very early in that initiative that the production of finished goods was not being allocated in a cost-effective manner. It appeared that new production was being awarded to the manufacturing plants of the other business unit, which had the most representation on our team, and the less prominent manufacturing plants were not being considered. Furthermore, production volume was constantly being transferred from less-represented sites to others without thorough and detailed evaluations.

A situation arose in which a project involving a new product launched in the European Union was awarded to the other business' largest manufacturing plant, which was located in the Czech Republic. When the basis for the decision was shared, it was evident that my business unit's less-prominent plant located in France, the country with one of the largest sales volumes for the product, was not included in the evaluation. When I asked why that manufacturing plant had not been considered, I was told it was because they did not have the capability. I was familiar with that plant and shared that my data did not align with that basis. The Product Supply Director, Jean Marc, informed me that he had visited the site and, as far as he was concerned, it was too expensive and not in scope. For perspective, I had worked on several very large and small capital projects with that plant over many years. Jean Marc took a one-day introductory trip to that plant and was, at that point, basically telling me, "*Trust me. I know better. This will not work.*" This was followed by a couple weeks of me having tough discussions with Jean Marc on the subject. Finally, he sent an email to me, which he deemed as his "final" position, stating that if I wanted to pursue an evaluation of the manufacturing plant in France, I was welcomed to do so, but I would be on my own and not sanctioned by the collaborative initiative. At that point, I dropped the discussion, and my push for a more diligent evaluation took second priority to other pressing issues.

One month later, I received a surprise email from Jean Marc's boss, Elvis, Chief Operating Officer, asking for a status of the evaluation of our manufacturing plant in France. I immediately called him on the phone and expressed my surprise at the request, considering his leadership team did not appreciate my recommendation to include France in the scope. Elvis apologized for the confusion and asked for an evaluation. I was elated at that news. However, my moment of joy was quickly erased by Elvis' condition. It was a problem. I had only five days to return with a cost, feasibility, and schedule - a process that normally took several weeks based on the scope. It felt like I was being asked to dry up the ocean with paper towels. As a leader, I chose to respond and step up to the challenge. I had to do it in a way that motivated, instilled confidence, and allowed my team to rally behind me. Because I am a praying man, I lifted up the surprise request to God for a miracle - and He did it!

I sent a fully detailed response back to Elvis and his team within the scheduled time frame. This was delivered, although I was given very minimal information and denied a conference call with the collaborative (*seriously*) initiative technical team to answer some basic questions.

Not only did our manufacturing plant in France have the necessary capability, but God also opened all kinds of doors to inspire, galvanize, and enable all the necessary functions in my business unit to drop other important work to focus on that request for one week. My R&D partners defined the formulation. My engineering team developed a detailed scope and documented a detailed capital estimate, and the team at the manufacturing plant completed a marathon of meetings to capture a manufacturing total delivered cost for each formula that would be produced. God did not stop there. Our plant's financials were so attractive that it came in better than the targeted financials of the project, which none of the other plants in the initial evaluation could deliver.

The Collaborative Initiative team did not believe the numbers and proceeded to challenge every line item in the capital estimate. At the end, the numbers stood against the onslaught of questions and critics and won the praise and recognition of Elvis and the rest of the Collaborative Team, except Jean Marc.

God came through in such a miraculous way that I could not explain how it all fell together in such a short period of time. For example, who would have known that one of the most critical chemicals in the formula was once used by the manufacturing plant in France but discontinued? The plant still had all the raw material handling equipment in place, as well as actual financials. They also still had a relationship with the supplier. This opened up a huge door of capabilities: lower capital, lower raw material cost, lower transportation cost, etc. It was a slam dunk!

Jean Marc and the Collaborative Initiative had no choice but to award the volume to the plant in France.

"Opportunity is missed by most people because it is dressed in overalls and looks like work." –Thomas Edison

God's Grace

Although I was good at my job, I acknowledged when divine intervention made me look like a great leader. My drive for diligence resulted in a more attractive project financial proposition for our business. And it took a herculean effort by a team of colleagues, who gave me favor and rose to the challenge. That was not because of me but all through the Grace of God.

Leadership Principles

1. In God we trust. All others must bring data.
2. Know when to push and when to back off.
3. Inspire an organization, and they will move mountains to deliver for the business.

Chapter 9

The Difficult Decision

> **Power Scripture:**
>
> *Trust in the Lord with all your heart and lean not on your own understanding; in all your ways submit to him, and he will make your paths straight.*
>
> Proverbs 3:5–6 (NIV)

Decision-Making (& Unconscious Bias)

Leaders make decisions. They look for the best available data to make the best decisions with the lowest risk to the business. Not every decision has the desired outcome. If it's forecasted to rain and you took your umbrella but it did not rain, did you make a good decision? Yes! Based on the data, your decision was sound, even though it did not rain. Great leaders go a step further and ensure these decisions are not influenced by unconscious bias. What if you were a man and had decided not to take your umbrella because you thought, "Men don't carry umbrellas." Was your decision sound? No! Because there was bias in your data driving you to make a poor decision. You were just lucky it did not rain. It is no more a good decision than racing a train to cross a track because you have a sports car. Bad idea!

Everyone carries some level of unconscious bias. It is influenced by our cultural backgrounds, personal experiences, and motivations. Great leaders are aware of their personal unconscious biases to others and work to eliminate them and not allow them to drive a decision that is not the best for the business.

Selecting someone who is less qualified over a more qualified candidate for a job because of a hurtful bias (such as race or gender) is wrong. Great leaders not only check for their own biases but also do not stand idly by while others demonstrate that unhealthy behavior to the organization. Would I have the courage to handle such a test, especially when it is systemic in an organization?

Early in my career, I transferred to the Valdosta manufacturing plant in Alabama and worked there for two years. A confidant shared with me that when I got to Valdosta, others were predicting that this transfer would be a disaster for me. I was a Black man in the South taking a technical leadership role leading the senior tenured all-white male group, who had been there from the start of that operation and had never had a Black team member or manager. They ran the plant. Managers were only successful if the technical team supported them. Then came . . . me.

In my initial meeting with the team, I spent most of the time allowing them to share their expectations of me. Next, I shared what I expected to do for them. I then made one request of them.

"Offer me the basic level of trust and respect you offer any average person," I said, "and increase or reduce that level of trust and respect accordingly to what I earn from you."

"You are assuming we trust and respect any manager other than the plant manager," joked Hinckley, the unofficial team leader. I still remember the group laughing and how uneasy my stomach felt.

Two years after that opening meeting, I was delivering record-breaking results and had a technical team that supported me, leaving me feeling truly empowered. However, we were now under-staffed, and our team needed to grow by one. I posted a new job opening to be filled internally. This was a coveted job. Therefore, as you can imagine, the applicants were many. Our team's superior results were also attractive to others who wanted to be part of a winning team. After many focused interviews and assessments, the field of applicants was finally reduced to the last two. One was a senior male from another department in the plant, and the other was a less tenured female also from another department.

The pressure and expectations from the plant population, especially from my technical team members, was that I must select the male candidate. There had just never been a woman in a technical job in the history of the plant. Of course, they reasoned that mechanical work is tough, requiring muscles and brute force. However, none of these were prerequisites for the job.

After the final interview, and once the candidate was gone, our selection team collectively breathed a deep sigh of relief. You could feel the whole team exhaling from the focused scrutiny we had done of each applicant's written information and intense interviews. We arose and tried to put order to the piles of candidate information, notes, empty coffee cups, crumbled candy bar wrappers, and intertwined laptop cables snaking their way across the table to their closest outlets.

"It's been a long day and week. Let's do a 10-minute cleanup and call it a day," I said. "We will do our assessment of the interviews and align on the best candidate tomorrow." Cleanup started before the last word was out of my mouth.

As usual, I stayed in the plant late in the evening to connect with the late shift and to catch up on other work that had been piling up on my desk. One of my technical team members on the late shift, Don, came to my office and asked if he could have a moment with me. Of course, I always have time for my team.

He placed a hand heavily on my shoulder, looked me straight in my eyes, and said with his deep southern drawl, "Kennedy, two years ago, none of us thought you would have lasted a year. We were going to eat you for lunch." There was a smile and a heavy stress on the word "eat." "But you were different from the start. Today, we have a situation." The smile vanished, and he continued. "You have no idea how the whole plant is waiting to see what your decision will be. We all know it is down to the last two candidates. I want to tell you to make the decision you think is right. Don't fear the reaction. In case you have not figured it out yet, we respect you more for doing what is right than what others want, and we have your back. OK? I gotta get back. Good night, boss." He released my shoulder and turned to leave.

"Thank you, Don," I said, "for caring enough and being courageous enough to share this coaching with me. You have no idea how empowering this is to me."

After he left, it dawned on me that I had been carrying a weight that I did not realize I carried. I had spent two years building a relationship with the plant, and at that point, I was about to make a decision that I knew could sever that relationship. Why? I had already done the analysis, and, though less tenured, the woman candidate had the best qualifications of all the candidates, both technically and organizationally. I was about to do what the plant influencers did not expect: promoting a woman into the technical team.

That night, I prayed and thanked God for sending an angel to encourage me to do the right thing. Had Don not talked with me, I would not have realized the value and impact of my decision until it was too late. I also asked God for courage to make the right decision, even though it was an unpopular one, and wisdom to guide my team and plant through this historical milestone. Change is inevitable but never easy. I prayed and asked God to help me be fair and to be an example of the following scripture verse: *"Stop judging by mere appearances, but instead judge correctly." John 7:24 (NIV).*

The following morning, our assessment team got together. I brought in breakfast for the team as a personal gift to thank them for their dedication. After a long discussion of everyone's assessments and recommendations, it was clear that, although the difference was razor thin, we had a divided team. I had the deciding vote. But I was prepared. Thank God for angels. We took a break.

After the break, I shared my understanding of what was at stake. I presented my position with the team that my desire was for us to all align on one recommendation versus me providing the deciding vote. I also shared that we had two guests coming to address us. It was Brian, the Plant Manager, and Geraldine, our Operating Department Manager. I had called both the night before to update them on our progress and to request their support for the outcome of the selection - whichever way it ended. I also asked them to address the selection team. Right at that moment, they came to the door of the conference room where we were gathered.

Brian went first. He shared his support and offered a few words on the historic nature of this selection, considering the fact that a woman was being considered for the job. Geraldine went next and shared her perspective and what it would mean for the benefit of the plant to have a woman on the technical team, if selected. They both pledged their full support of whatever decision the selection team aligned on. I prayed that their visit met my intent, which was to bring some level of comfort and support to the selection team.

After the brass left, I shared my perspective on the information they presented and provided some clarifications. I closed by asking a "What has to be true . . ." question. At the end, the whole team agreed to support one decision: to promote the woman candidate. We spent the next couple hours on the appropriate communication, the method of communication, and the coordination of this important communication to the different departments in the plant. The time we took to craft the communication plan was invaluable. It included how we would manage and support folks who would be in different stages of the change cycle after the message went out.

After the announcements, I braced myself for tough feedback and cold shoulders. There were a few. However, I was stunned at the other responses. An overwhelming number of folks shook my hand, gave me hugs and high-fives, and patted me on the back for making the hard decision and sticking to doing what was right. The technical team leaders from the three operating departments and the administrative group told me this was not the decision they would have made but thanked me for making what they acknowledged as the right one. Of course, not everyone was happy with the outcome. No surprise there.

Finally, the selection team gave me feedback as a team, with the guy who was the least supportive speaking on behalf of the team. He shared how impressed they were with the process, stated that this was the most transparent process they had experienced, and expressed how glad they were to work with me. Yep. That one brought a tear or two. I attributed that to me just being emotionally exhausted at that time!

"What separates talented people in the end is the courage to make the really hard call. A lot of hard calls are not tough because they are hard to figure out. They are tough because they have short-term sacrifice or emotional content that people don't want to deal with. It's human nature to avoid that kind of pain." –A.G. Lafley, Former P&G CEO

God's Grace

As I look back, one thing was clear. This decision did not come about because I was so great. God placed me in a situation, led me to an opportunity, provided an angel to help guide me through this difficult decision, and gave me supportive and empowering leaders in my Plant Manager and Operating Department Manager and a team that was receptive to change. I call that God's Grace!

Leadership Principles

1. Change is inevitable.
2. Leading change takes courage.
3. The greatest leaders do what is right versus what is comfortable.

Chapter 10

Enabling Success

Power Scripture:

But he said to me, "My grace is sufficient for you, for my power is made perfect in weakness." Therefore, I will boast all the more gladly of my weakness, so that the power of Christ may rest upon me.

2 Corinthians 12:9 (ESV)

Empowerment

Good leaders will ensure their employees *are* empowered and *feel* empowered. There is a very good chance that if you send me to an unknown place and give me no directions that I will get lost. That will make me frustrated, and I will not be able to meet your needs. Similarly, sending an individual on a task without being empowered can result in failure and frustration.

Empowering an individual is giving them the tools they need to be successful. This means sharing needed resources such as information, funds, and staffing, as well as ensuring that they have the knowledge by providing training and that they have the authority and confidence to deliver. In other words, they need to have all the right tools - power and authority - to be successful in whatever they need to deliver.

Empowerment is not a feeling. It is a state of being. However, when someone "feels" empowered, they can demonstrate a high level of autonomy and motivation in making decisions that are beneficial to the organization. Empowerment drives ownership. Ownership drives accountability and loyalty, which translates to delivering breakthrough results, as in the following situation.

My first four years with the company was in the corporate offices. I then transferred to one of our manufacturing plants. I learned that I loved working in a plant. Don't get me wrong. I enjoyed taking a technical project from concept to equipment installation and seeing the process through or packaging equipment operate as designed. But there is something special about receiving the raw materials that go into making and packaging the product. It was awesome to touch the finished cases of products going out from the distribution center. There is a sense of pride in seeing a product from my manufacturing plant on store shelves at Walmart, Target, Sam's Club, Costco, and other retail and club stores. I would walk down the store aisle fixing the presentation of our company products. I would amaze my kids by telling them a great deal about a product just by looking at the code date.

I loved the people of the manufacturing plant, especially my technical team. I loved my work family, my friends, and the culture. One never knew what challenges they would walk into when they got to the plant each morning. Our team was proud that whatever the technical problem, we could solve it. And if it could not be solved right now, we would *MacGyver* a patch job to keep the plant running. After all, that's what we did . . . fix things that broke down. We were heroes. Others in the plant saw us as heroes. We lived to be called to fix equipment breakdowns.

This was all great until I attended a seminar by W. Edwards Deming on total quality. I started understanding the concepts of reliability and maintenance management. I realized that the culture of rushing from one crisis to the next - like heroes to save the day rather than fixing it right the first time - was actually costing our company more money. We really should have been working ourselves out of the job of fixing things.

Fresh from the seminar, I posed a question to my senior technical team member. "Harvey, what if we never had a breakdown?" He looked at me puzzled. I repeated, "What would you do if the process never had a failure?" He realized I was serious and started laughing.

While laughing, he shouted over the hum of the operation to the lead process technician running the process operation, looking for support. "Hey, Brian! Germo here wants to know what we would do if the plant ran nonstop without mechanical problems!" Germo was the affectionate name they called me.

Brian cracked back, "Well, I could make a lot more product for P&G to sell, and maybe you guys could work on some of my ideas to improve things around here!" I could not believe how perfect this response was! I latched onto Brian's response and started developing my vision to be shared at our upcoming mechanical team offsite meeting.

I presented my thoughts on the purpose of our team at our next team offsite meeting. I also shared what it was not. It was not to be "grease monkeys." I presented my perspective that this was not just a mechanical team, as we were called, but a technical team of leaders with the responsibility to ensure the process operation was reliable for today's needs and, in a state of continuous improvement, to deliver more to our business for tomorrow's needs. I shared the basis for my perspective.

I proposed changing the team's name from the "Making Department Mechanical Team" to the "Making Department Technical Team." I offered that the new name better reflected our focus on overall maintenance for reliability as well as continuous improvement rather than just breakdown maintenance. The team members were intrigued by the prospect of getting into other areas of interest and started sharing ideas they had for improvements. Then, there was the request for a bigger budget to get the right tools if I wanted them to do more than "maintain."

Building on their energy, I decided to sweeten the deal. I offered a challenge. The team had complained before that they had requested proper tools and equipment from my predecessors but were always told there was no budget - hence their push for a bigger budget to get some tools. As a challenge, I offered that if they were able to make our process more capable by reducing breakdowns and improving its reliability, which would result in a reduction of how much we spent on spare parts, then I would allow them to spend ten percent of the savings on their shop for tools.

"You could do that?" one team member asked.

"Sure!" I replied.

"And we can spend it on whatever tools we need?"

"Yes. If the tool is required to repair, maintain, or improve the operation. No going off the deep end." I laughed. They perked up in their chairs.

"I'm taking notes!" declared Arthur. And the whole team laughed. What happened following that meeting was a miracle.

The following week, Arthur installed a nicely designed poster over the maintenance shop, which read, "Making Department Technical Team Workshop." It drew a lot of attention. It was always referred to as the "Shop" or the "Mechanical Shop" in the past. A few days later, Arthur approached me about a meeting.

"Germo," he said. "Is it okay if we schedule a meeting with you later this week?" These guys disliked meetings with a passion, so for them to call me into a meeting was significant and, while I had my suspicion of what this could be about, I was not about to say, "No!"

"Absolutely!" I responded. "May I ask what the meeting is about?"

Arthur smiled and said, "We have a proposal we want to share with you."

"A proposal? What kind of proposal?" I asked, grinning from ear to ear because I just knew that my team asking to share a proposal with me could only mean another request for money to spend on tools. I could just imagine them coming up with a creative way to get tools that were not in the budget.

Arthur smiled and said, "I know what you are thinking, and no, it's not for new tools - although we do need some." He could not help throwing that in. "It's a proposal for our new shop. And we hope you like it!"

"Wait. What new shop?" I asked, as my face instinctively displayed my surprise by my raised eyebrows and widened eyes. "That is worse than asking for tools!" I exclaimed, thinking out loud.

"It's not what you think," Arthur said, placing one hand firmly on my shoulder and looking over his spectacles like a father to a concerned child. "We have a plan we think you will like, so please don't sweat over it. OK?" His seriousness quieted my emotions and brought on anticipation.

"OK," I responded. "Now I can hardly wait for the meeting!"

On the day of the meeting, when I got to the scheduled conference room, the team was already there. They had an air of excitement about them. Arthur began by unrolling a drawing. It was the floorplan of what their renovated Technical Team Workshop should look like in six months. It was completed with color schemes and labels and markings for equipment placement, including a new lathe.

As it turned out, Arthur was also an architect. He came up with the idea and drew up the plan as their inspiration. Needless to say, I was thoroughly impressed. My team was more talented than I had imagined. They just needed to be supported and empowered!

All eyes turned to Arthur, who was now clearly the spokesman for this project.

"We are a proud group of southern boys, and we are going to deliver against your challenge," he started. I liked how he'd started! "What you are looking at is our plan to reward ourselves with a nice upgrade to our shop and make it more fun to work around here. We would like you to approve us using our ten percent savings to fund this project. Remember, you said that Mr. What's-his-name said we need to clean things up and get back to how it was designed to be."

"Mr. What's-his-name's name is 'Deming,'" I corrected him. "And yes. I did share that you should get the equipment back to base condition to be able to see the oil leaks, drips, and other defects."

Jim, the junior member, jumped in. "Well, that's what we are proposing here with the shop. And not a dime comes out of your budget. It'll all be from our savings when we improve the equipment reliability results." I was truly amazed at this group of talented technical leaders, and I was blessed to be their leader. I never felt prouder of them.

My thoughts paused when the team suddenly stopped talking and all eyes were on me. "Yes. You have my approval." I smiled. "What do you need from me to help you see your vision come alive?" I asked. Jim already had something typed up. The first request was for me to share more of what I'd learned from the Deming seminar. I could hardly contain myself. *Thank You, Lord!* I said to myself.

I spent the next two weeks training and coaching, using simple one-idea lessons on what I had learned about root cause analysis and other concepts of maintenance management. Each lesson focused on only one point. It made it easy to digest and to do it in only ten minutes during our daily huddles. As requested, I had to double back to the manufacturing plant each evening to catch my team members who were working the late shift. Also, we already had a regularly scheduled all-plant maintenance event where we would shut down the operation and complete needed repairs and other installations. We started using that event as an opportunity to make improvements that would last versus quick fixes.

Over the next few months, I allowed the team to purchase a few much-needed tools and equipment to tackle some of the new challenges they were facing. They even purchased an office label maker to label some of the equipment.

I assigned Harvey, the team influencer, as the czar for the initiative. He liked his title and took his job very seriously, encouraging the team and making requests of me to remove barriers in their way. He was able to communicate to the others in ways I could not. We saw our equipment runtime steadily improve.

Our daily morning shift overlap meeting became a war room chasing after root causes, so we fixed a problem once so we wouldn't have to touch it again. Jim started plotting our runtime on a whiteboard in our team room with "DO NOT ERASE" scribbled on it. A couple months into the challenge and that board became the first thing to be checked in the morning by others in the department to see how our team was doing. The idea of increasing runtime started catching on like a virus.

By the end of our fiscal year, our operation had broken all kinds of records - not only in reliability but also in safety. Incredibly, the more reliably we operated, the fewer injuries we experienced. Three months later, we dedicated a sparkling, newly painted Technical Team Workshop, complete with a team room for training and a technical documentation area for equipment files, schematics, and vendor catalogues. The Making Department Technical Workshop had become a showcase of the plant for leaders and dignitaries who were visiting the site.

The team gave me an appreciation at our Making Department Technical Team's Christmas event. They shared that, of all their managers, I was one of the few who treated them like the principle that this manufacturing plant was built on: a high-performance organization. They explained that they did not know what it was about me, but they knew they could trust me and that I was a man of my word. This gave them the desire to take up my challenge, even though they did not think it was possible. And when Arthur came up with his layout of what the shop could look like, it got them too excited not to try. The first time they broke their operation runtime record, everyone in the plant was talking about it, and that just gave them even more incentive to keep at it.

God's Grace

Grace is defined as unmerited favor. When I took leadership of the team, I was not supposed to be successful, by all expectations. Even my team expected me to fail within the first year. But God gave me favor in their eyes faster than I could prove myself.

I gave them the challenge when I was less than a year into the job. And the trust and respect they gave me - you would think I had been working with them for many years. I know if it had not been for the Grace of God, I would not have been successful, much less able to make transformational change amongst the toughest group of guys who had been working together for decades.

Leadership Principles

1. An empowered team will break records.
2. An empowered team is a motivated team.
3. Respect builds trust.

Chapter 11

Take Action

Bias for Action

As a great leader, you must demonstrate a bias for action. Action generates results. Inaction is usually a result of corporate swirl, where it takes forever to get a decision made.

A bias for action means calculated risks are taken even in the presence of uncertainty, and decisions are made quickly to deliver the desired result in a timely fashion. There are times when it is right to do due diligence and complete a detailed investigation before a decision is made. There are also occasions when time is not on your side and to make progress, you have to take action with unconventional solutions to solve unconventional problems. A leader with a bias for action never quits or gives up when conventional solutions fail. A leader with a bias for action sees this as an invitation and an opportunity to dive deep into the unconventional playing field.

Someone who does not have a bias for action will tend to get stuck when challenged with uncertainty or when conventional solutions fail. They can become stuck at three different times. They can get stuck trying to define the problem correctly, which is usually due to biases, or in the research, due to a lack of transformational understanding. They tend to get stuck in the process and go into a tailspin due to a never-ending analysis. They also have the tendency to prolong analysis and research to a point of diminishing returns, usually in the name of perfection. This is what we affectionately refer to as "analysis paralysis." Finally, they will get stuck in the ending phase due to always seeing an improvement that "should" be made.

A project is dead on arrival if your back is against the wall and a leader cannot define the problem, engages in analysis paralysis, or is never ready to move forward with the best-known solution. Such times call for quick decisions and intentional actions. The following situation is an example where our backs were against the wall, the clock was ticking, and our technical challenge did not have a conventional solution. But we had to take action!

Very few capital projects are executed with no issues. The higher the complexity of a project, the higher the risk of challenges. Midway through my career, one of my capital projects flowing out of the innovation pipeline checked every box on the complexity spectrum. It was a new-to-the-world product. It was a new form of product to my business, which routinely dealt with other forms like granules, pastes, and liquids.

The equipment process to manufacture this new product did not exist on the market. It required a high level of equipment innovation. The product had outperformed every expectation, breaking records in consumer tests. This was a winner. It had already won internal recognition for its innovation and would surely win external awards.

The product made it through many evaluation gates and was carrying some risks, but there were plans to mitigate them. Nothing unusual. However, over time, we started carrying more risks than the technical team felt comfortable with, and the push was on from our business leaders. There were technical challenges with the equipment to make the product that we were having difficulty solving. There was progress against these risks, but progress was small and slow coming.

The technical team proposed a delay in the project. The counterproposal by our managers was to stay on track, and a newly formed interdisciplinary Task Force would help with the risk management. That task force was made up of senior leaders specifically for this project. The plan was to meet every

Friday with the task force to review progress against our risk mitigation plan.

"And oh, by the way," our marketing director said, "product launch was already committed to our key retail customers." That meant no going back. We had to find solutions.

The next few weeks were not pretty. We were marching down a path with red flags flying on both sides of the path. We involved highly respected resources internally and externally, including academia, to help us get to the fundamental transformations we needed to understand and solve these challenges with some success.

Finally, eight weeks before launch, I had to declare the undesirable news that there was no way the process equipment would work. Engineering did not have a solution. All of our equipment tests were producing unpredictable results. At that point, I assumed my career was in the balance.

What followed was two weeks of intense project reviews between the commercial and technical leadership teams. We all agreed that our backs were against the wall with commitments already made to our commercial customers. We decided that the engineering and research & development functions needed to design and install a process, even if it was fully manual, to produce enough product to launch. In parallel, we would continue to address the risks. We had to keep driving toward a solution.

I latched onto a scripture verse that says, *"Don't burn out; keeping yourselves fueled and aflame. Be alert servants of the Master, cheerfully expectant. Don't quit in hard times; pray all the harder. Help needy Christians; be inventive in hospitality." Romans 12:11–13 (MSG).*

We now had six weeks to launch. Besides a miracle, I needed to ensure my leadership supported my bias for action. Swirl-around decisions and authorizations were not an option. I prayed the kind of prayer that you pray when you really need a miracle.

It was six weeks from innovation to startup of a process we had already been working on for years. Something different was needed. I asked my engineering leader for the green light to take increased calculated risks and funding in order to pull in any resource I wanted. I delegated my other critical projects to my senior team members who were not on this particular project. This allowed me to give this innovation my full, one hundred and fifty percent attention.

I pulled in a small group of inventors we had in our business to help identify an unconventional solution. They knew how to break every rule in physics to brainstorm some wild ideas based on the transformations we needed. We quickly zeroed in on a couple of options that could work.

At that point, I invited a small upstream technology development company to join our team. I had met the owner at a recent packaging conference in Chicago. Incidentally, their facility was located close to our engineering laboratory. They were also a design & fabrication shop. After a couple meetings with them, we selected the design concept most probable to be successful. They created a plan to fabricate the design in large modules of the packaging line to enable plug and play at installation. We made the decision to continue with all of our raw material procurement. *Five weeks left.*

The next two weeks were filled with small wins as we resolved one barrier after another, giving the team motivation that we could possibly make this miracle work. *Three weeks left.*

We started fabricating and testing equipment unit operations in parallel as we progressed. It was working as intended. But we needed more manual labor than desired. The personnel safety team went to work to update the personnel safety plan with an ergonomic plan. Quality tests were being done to ensure our specifications were not being compromised. *One week to go.*

We started final preparation of the installation site, as well as integrating and testing the full equipment to confirm everything worked. Test results were positive. We took Friday night off. *One weekend to go.*

That Saturday morning, the equipment modules were secured on a flatbed truck for the long drive to the installation site. On Sunday afternoon, the equipment was offloaded at the manufacturing plant. The equipment was installed overnight Sunday. The modular design paid off - it was like putting Lego® blocks together. Equipment setup and testing were a breeze. We knew every bolt on that machine. We were virtually married to that machine 24/7 for several weeks, only taking time for naps and changes of clothes. At least, that's how it felt.

By noon on Monday, we were making the product. The process of making the product was semi-automatic, and packaging was fully manual, which was okay for now. We produced enough quality samples to ship to our key commercial customers on schedule. We had met our commitment, and I was exhausted. I had just led my engineering team through a miracle!

God's Grace

When I looked at the award I was given (I carried that trophy into retirement), I knew I had the Grace of God on me. I could not have made all the circumstances fall into place, going from idea generation to startup, in six weeks. This process normally takes anywhere from several months to a couple years. So, God blessed me to have a team of "Einsteins" right at my fingertips and a development vendor with a design/fab shop who was hungry for my business less than 20 miles from my office and with the capability to pull this off.

I was also blessed with leadership that challenged me to do the impossible and a team who was willing to follow my lead down a path they saw as an adventure. Yes, they thought I was crazy, but they were willing to give it a shot. We had no time for inaction. God gave me favor, which resulted in success.

Leadership Principles

1. If you are the leader, lead versus manage.
2. Be open to try unconventional ideas to overcome unconventional challenges.
3. Be willing to make the tough call.

Chapter 12

Be Courageous

> ### Power Scripture:
>
> *"Go and get all the Jews living in Susa together. Fast for me. Don't eat or drink for three days, either day or night. I and my maids will fast with you. If you will do this, I'll go to the king, even though it's forbidden. If I die, I die."*
>
> *Esther 4:16 (MSG)*

Courageous Leadership

Understand that courage does not mean that you have no fear. Courage is actually doing something in the presence of fear. It is not barging in like a bull in a china shop fearlessly. It has purpose and direction. It is persisting through uncomfortable situations. When the going gets tough, courageous leaders keep making progress. Courageous leaders lead from the front. They do what is needed to energize their followers, treat them fairly, protect them fiercely from external forces, and empower them to do their jobs with confidence.

Organizations with courageous leaders deliver exceptional results. Courageous leaders are unbiased and intentionally focused. They are authentic, seek feedback, foster collaboration, encourage creativity, master change, have integrity, and demonstrate empathy.

Courageous leaders have a "leading up" philosophy. It is not about "pleasing the boss." It is about taking some of the burden off your leader's shoulders. It is about working with hierarchy and assisting them to make informed decisions by providing transparent communication courageously.

Something else courageous leaders do very well: face uncomfortable, crucial conversations head on. They will initiate the difficult conversation and work through it with authenticity. That conversation is exponentially difficult when you are confronting your boss. In my situation, I had to summon a level of courage I had never known before. The other end of that conversation was not my boss but my boss's boss.

My manufacturing plant was in the process of an organizational renewal. It was determined that for us to ensure a culture poised to deliver the next level of breakthrough results, we needed to assess and change some things. There were two key drivers. First, the company was asking for more, and second, thanks to a sizable group of transferees from another plant, there was a groundswell of demands driving an unhealthy culture.

My plant's organization was designed with a Technician Leadership Culture, and the transferees were from union plants.

Although there are benefits to both a union as well as a non-union culture, this plant was designed and structured to be run based on a leadership and team culture.

I was not on the official Plant Leadership Team (PLT), but due to my job, I had a lot of influence with the plant employees. I believe that was the driver for me being offered to join the PLT to help with the organizational restructuring efforts.

My first recommendation to the PLT was to involve one representative technician leader from each of our four departments. Culture is the hardest to change, and without input from the technicians, this would be worse than an uphill battle - more like pushing a wet noodle up a hill. That recommendation received complete support - or so I thought.

Halfway through the design, I started noticing a disturbing pattern. Important decisions that were made when the technician leaders were with us would be revisited and most often changed when they were not in the meeting. The justification given to the technicians was that they had more data and had been forced to make a quick decision but that the essence of what we had agreed upon was not lost. That may have been partially true for any individual decision. However, in aggregate, it had a compounding effect, and the result was far from the original intent.

I discussed my concern with a few other managers who were on the leadership team and got confirmation of my concern. It was clear that Mathias, our Plant Manager, was set in his vision of the solution he wanted, versus allowing the process to determine the outcome.

And everyone seemed to be playing the political game. I tried to fall into line.

It would not be long after that the technicians in the PLT started noticing the issue and approached me with their concerns. They asked me to join them for lunch one day. I knew what it was about.

"We have a problem and need your advice, Kennedy," said Johnny before I could even sit down. Johnny was one of the more vocal members, and he did not mince words. "We feel that PLT is just using us to say they have technician input, but that is not true. We really do not feel like we are a part of the team, and we think it is best if we get off."

"But we wanted to see if you think we are crazy or have any ideas for us, because you are also on the team," chimed in Suzie while giving Johnny a sideways glance that said, "Cool down!"

"What did I say?" defended Johnny. "I'm just saying what y'all are afraid to say!"

"We should not be on the team if our input is not being valued," said Bob, the senior among the group.

"But we don't want to come across as being disgruntled. You know what I mean?" added Suzie.

The discussion went on for a short while. I affirmed their courage and the great leadership behaviors they had demonstrated. I then gave them coaching on how to summarize their concerns and any recommendation on one clear and concise page and to be prepared to share it in our next meeting. Because they had approached me in confidence, I did not share our discussion with anyone.

I was impressed at the next meeting. The technicians had asked for and were granted time on our agenda. They shared their one-page summary of observations and concerns. They ended with a recommendation that they step out from the PLT and, instead, be used as "consultants" on an "as-needed" basis. I thought that was very innovative thinking!

Mathias acknowledged that there were several changes to decisions we had made with them. He then asked them to stay on the team and said that we would work to keep future changes to a minimum. We did the contrary. And there were several moves Mathias made that were outside of the design. Some were a little hard for me to stomach. All the other team members who were higher than me in the organization knew what was going on and talked about it. No one was confronting Mathias.

When I found I could not, in good faith, support a design that was not a result of our process but that of our leader's opinion (rather than data), I had to make a choice. I needed to have a crucial conversation - and it was not with a peer or subordinate.

Managing up is easier when the stakes are low. It is exponentially more challenging when it involves giving feedback, especially to your boss's boss. But I know that *"For the Spirit God gave us does not make us timid, but gives us power, love and self-discipline." 2 Timothy 1:7 (NIV).*

I prayed about what I should do. I set up a meeting with Mathias to provide feedback and a decision I had taken. This was not an easy task, as I had never given structured constructive feedback to anyone one level above me - let alone two levels above me - in the company before.

I set up to meet in the cafeteria over coffee. A neutral place. His office was just way too intimidating. Subject? Coaching. I expected him to naturally assume I was asking for some coaching. I was nervous. No backing out now. I documented what I was going to share with him so that I would not deviate from my message. Did I say I was nervous?

The day before the meeting, I was so nervous that I needed some mental reinforcement. So, I dragged my office buddy, Glenda, to the cafeteria for the cup of coffee she did not know she needed. There, I shared my plan so that she would tell me I was about to commit career suicide and that I should cancel the meeting with Mathias. She did not.

"OK. I'm going to ignore the part about you requesting a transfer back to Cincinnati for now. But this is very courageous, Kennedy!" Glenda said.

"You are supposed to say that to make me feel brave," I replied. "I believe it is more like career suicide! And you are the first to know of my wish to move back to Cincinnati, so keep it between us."

"You know me. I would tell you if you were being crazy," she correctly fired back with a huge grin on her face. "Just get to the cafeteria ahead of the meeting, so you can have a chance to get relaxed and ready for him to show up." The grin faded.

"Good advice. Thanks," I whispered. "Just pray for me," I continued. "I'm nervous at just the thought of having this meeting, but I know that I must do what is right."

"And that's why you are being courageous," she said with a smile. Sitting back in her chair, Glenda suddenly seemed "older and wiser."

I decided not to share the meeting with my boss. I was about to give his boss some feedback, and I was sure he would not approve of it. However, I felt a need to do something, and this, to me, was the right approach, politically correct or not, and hopefully I would still have a job at the end.

I went to the cafeteria early, as planned, so I could relax before the meeting. Well, guess who was already in the cafeteria drinking coffee? The blessing was that I did not have time to get butterflies in my tummy. I got my coffee and joined Mathias at the table.

After a quick greeting and some small talk, I pulled out my one-pager.

"Mathias," I started. "I would like to thank you for agreeing to meet with me. I would like to share with you some observations and recommendations, as well as a decision I have made. However, I am asking that you please listen and allow me to completely finish my prepared comments before jumping in. Would that be OK?" Gulp! No turning back now!

"Absolutely!" Mathias said with his usual wide grin and piercing blue eyes while leaning forward with both elbows on the table. He started rubbing his hands together like he could hardly wait for the juicy part of a big piece of gossip. His slender frame all of a sudden seemed larger.

I started by thanking him for his support and belief in me enough to invite me to join the PLT and participate in the organization's redesign. I shared that he was a strong leader with a clear path on what he wanted for the plant. I told him I concluded his leadership style was vastly different from my style. Not right nor wrong, just different. I then shared that I could not, in good faith, continue to represent the PLT with a message that we designed and were about to implement an organization change that had input from the shop floor when I had not seen that happen. Instead, I recommended three things: first, that he would be more authentic with the PLT and share what he really wanted to do; second, that he would demonstrate that he valued the technician leaders' input more by showing them how he had incorporated their input; third, that he trusted the organization assessment and design work process to deliver what we needed versus forcing it to do what he wanted. Finally, I shared that I had decided I would pray for a successful rollout but would not be there for it because I wanted to be transferred back to Cincinnati.

Then, I waited for the shoe to drop. But it did not.

With a broad smile on his face, Mathias, who had settled back in his chair by now, wiggled while leaning forward again and said, "Kennedy, thank you very much for this gift. You have no idea how much I appreciate the feedback or how courageous that was. I value leaders around me who are not afraid to tell me when I am wrong. I may not agree, but that is okay. I want us to have the conversation. You have certainly developed professionally since joining the plant."

"Whew! Thank you, and yes, I was nervous," I exclaimed, while trying to calm my knees that were knocking under the table.

Mathias asked me if there were any killer issues I saw and whether I had any suggestions on how we could resolve them. I offered a few areas I thought would be dead on arrival among the plant employees and that would definitely serve as fire to those who were already unhappy with the plant having that type of Technician Leadership Culture. I suggested his PLT do a SWOT (Strength - Weakness - Opportunity - Threat) analysis of the design we were creating. Finally, I suggested he lead a separate peer review with the technician leaders who were on our team for their input and suggestions. That would be a huge deposit in their emotional bank accounts.

Mathias was concerned the technicians would have a false sense that what they recommended must be implemented. I suggested being authentic and sharing with them that their input would be considered but that he could not guarantee it would all be implemented. And that if it was not adopted, Mathias or one of the other managers would close the loop with them.

"They just want to know their input is valued, Mathias. They already know most of their input is just that - input to be considered. They value the opportunity to give their perspective and share their experiences. Their ideas do not have to be implemented, but they should be authentically considered," I said.

He then said he had one final request. "Would you delay your relocation until after the design implementation and rollout? I value your approach and the trust the technicians have in you."

My Plant Manager did put his money where his mouth was at the next PLT meeting. He did not mention our conversation - thank God - but apologized and asked for input on what we would do differently to make the design better reflect the results of our assessment. The input from the rest of the team was like opening up a floodgate. Seven months later, Mathias approved my relocation and promoted me to the next job band level for my contributions.

"Efforts and courage are not enough without purpose and direction."
–John F. Kennedy

God's Grace

During the culture change, God gave me a high level of favor with the technicians, even those I did not directly work with. That made our implementation a little easier. God also turned around what would have been a bad situation for me and gave me a favor with my Plant Manager. This could have been very different if God's Hands were not on my life.

Leadership Principles

1. Be courageous but objective.
2. Be authentic.
3. Managing up takes courage.

Chapter 13

Progress-Focused

Risk-Taking

Taking risks in business is about making decisions where the outcome is uncertain or unpredictable but where there is a chance or probability that the outcome will be favorable. The reverse is also true. There is a probability the outcome will not be favorable and something undesirable or bad can happen.

Often, when someone thinks of taking risks, the focus is on the negative. Something bad might happen. We are wired that way for self-preservation, especially if it involves a risk of getting hurt or injured. Then there are those of us who love the adrenaline rush associated with taking a chance on something that could go drastically wrong. One example is racing to cross railroad tracks ahead of the hurling mass of steel with one hundred freight cars coming at us with no time at all to brake and avoid being crushed. A life lost is not worth the risk. Even if you made it across the tracks, that would still have been a careless, irresponsible, and drastically poor decision.

A leader does not take careless risks and put the business in a compromising position by poor risk calculations. However, a prudent leader who is a risk-taker always weighs the options to determine the appropriate course of action. If the benefit outweighs the risk, it most likely is worth taking the risk. If success does not come, it was still worth taking the chance. In other words, if it was forecasted to rain and I walked with my umbrella, it would still have been a good decision, even if it did not rain.

In my situation, the risk of failure was extremely high, but the benefits of success were even higher. In this case, leadership empowered us to make the decisions, understanding the risks, and was willing to absorb failure.

I was tasked with leading a project to reintroduce a product into the Asia-Pacific market. The product was initially discontinued in the market for various reasons. So, the product needed to be reformulated. This meant it potentially also needed new raw materials, maybe process equipment changes, new artwork . . . the list goes on and on. However, I did not see that as a challenge. To me, it was a simple and routine capital project execution; but that was before I was given a timeline, which was only twenty-five percent of what a typical project like this would normally require from project kickoff to startup.

Having lost count on my execution of such projects and my project management experience, I calmly shared the basis for a timeline that was more feasible and that was an estimate, which would be better defined once I met with the multifunctional team to develop a critical path schedule. The response from Gasper, our business leader, did not sit well with a few of my team members who had also been in that meeting. Thank God we had been on a conference call.

"I understand your process," Gasper said, "but the given date is not negotiable. It's being driven by the market."

I had just joined the organization, and, at that point, I thought I had made my worst career move. Following the earth-shattering conference call, I had two priorities: get my new team emotionally settled and discuss expectations with my new business leader.

My message to my team was that everyone wants to be great and because our company hires the best and brightest, Gasper must have a rational motivation driving his request and position. I asked my team to allow me time to understand that motivation before we reacted. I then scheduled a call with Gasper to understand the drivers for what seemed like an impossible request of an experienced and dedicated technical team.

The meeting was held. Gasper understood my request for clarification of the compelling business need. The goal post did not move. Instead, he asked, "What needs to be true to deliver this project?"

I thought for a moment, then replied nonchalantly, "You have to be okay with seventy-eight percent done rather than one hundred percent perfect; and even then, I can deliver the project, but with only a twenty-five percent confidence level, assuming you are willing to walk away from that investment if the formula or process equipment does not work."

"I'll take it. I'll be the approver of any decision that is difficult for the team or that requires a delay," he answered. I almost fell off my chair. "Also, if you are okay with it, invite me to your project kickoff so I can help set expectations," he continued. "I want the team to feel okay with breaking the process paradigms and artificial guard rails we have established." No debate from me. I accepted the offer to help with the messaging to the team but not before stressing the huge risk being intentionally injected into the project.

I called my team together for a debrief of my meeting with Gasper. Before starting the meeting, I wrote on the white board: "78% done is better than 100% perfect." My icebreaker at the start of the meeting was a simple question: "What does that (what I wrote) mean to you?" We exhausted a rich dialogue on my question. Some of the answers were:

- It's better to just get it done versus spinning your wheels trying to get it perfect.

- Perfection commands a cost, and it may not drive any profit.

- I may be OK with it not being perfect.

- Sometimes you have to move forward with what you have.

- A bird in the hand is worth two in the bush.

Of course, considering the situation and the request, some of my team members did not think this was funny. The fact that we were entertaining a question surrounding not striving to be the best was very anti-P&G culture. Some offered sarcastic comments like:

"Hallelujah, we are going to compromise!"

"We are going to play in the less-than-premium space for a change. Will we charge less-than-premium prices?"

"Sooooo . . . we are settling to be less than perfect," said my senior product supply team member, lengthening his "so" for effect.

"You can never be one hundred percent perfect, so this statement is difficult to support," said one of my analytical friends.

One member asked why seventy-eight percent versus a "nice" round number. I explained it was random, but I used a number that would force a conversation. I did not stifle the brainstorming session but allowed the team to comment freely.

Following the icebreaker, I summarized the outcome of my meeting with Gasper. I shared the business drivers for the impossible schedule and that our leadership was willing to take the risk, knowing that there was a very low probability of success in delivering the project. The opportunity was for us to define a solution in order to deliver a project, which currently only had a twenty-five percent probability of success. I explained that our leadership understood the risks but was willing to make the investment knowing the throwaway costs might be high. If the gamble paid off, the return would be record-breaking for the business model both in the short and long term. I explained that in this case, we had to try our best to deliver, knowing there would be times when we would have to settle for less than perfect or be willing to make a decision without all the input.

However, for clarity, I reminded the team that compromising on product quality, safety, or any legal requirements was not an option. I did all I could to motivate that team of *perfectionists* to think differently and be okay with not being greater than ninety-five percent confident on a result. I asked the members to meet with their respective employees and be prepared for our kickoff meeting where we would complete our plan of action. By the end of the meeting, there was nervous excitement about the challenge ahead. Everyone headed to their offices. I went to find a quiet place. As I always did before all my projects - but especially challenging ones - I went to God in prayer.

The project kickoff meeting went better than expected. It was good that Gasper called in to the meeting, but it turned out to not be necessary. The team was already revved up to drive forward. I took the team through a day of creating and streamlining the path forward, not the typical flow of presentations as was customary during large capital project team kickoff meetings.

The project progressed in organized chaos. It became a process of defining the risks, being clear on all available assumptions, and driving parallel, critical path schedules for activities we would normally do in series. If one path did not work, we would quickly pivot to another option. Leadership team meetings happened in our team room using the marked-up paper on the walls or straight from our laptops. The agenda would be scribbled on the whiteboard versus a nice handout. Our leadership appreciated our creativity.

Whatever our approach, we did not compromise on generating the right data. Process gates simply became milestones rather than decision points. The issues list was long. The project reviews were intense - sometimes too intense. Decision-making was quick after multiple times of reminding the team members that they were not the ultimate approvers of a critical decision we would be debating.

One of my coaches gave me blunt feedback after it looked like I was being side-tracked by passionate discussions.

"Kennedy," she said, "don't you think you would make more progress if you all mixed your emotions with data?"

"You are right. It's open season on opinions but hard to debate facts," I agreed. It was nothing I did not know. But sometimes we need a coach to remind us of the obvious.

I had direct access to our business leadership. The team learned to stop debating issues that we could easily elevate to Gasper and our marketing manager for a quick decision. In many cases, we were amazed at some of the alignments we received to proceed. In one case, we overnighted raw material from Asia to the manufacturing plant in the United States, even before we received the raw materials quality test results. We would have never done that on a normally executed project - but this was not normal. It called for taking calculated risks, being okay with being uncomfortable, and allowing leadership to make the critical decisions when needed versus being "self-designated" gatekeepers.

The project also called for an unprecedented collaboration among all functions, including manufacturing, from project kickoff to product launch. When one of the new raw materials required special handling, a manufacturing team member came up with a simple temporary solution to get us through the first production cycle. The permanent solution would be designed later, freeing that engineer to move on to another critical issue. Every step of the way was grueling. It challenged every one of our paradigms on a capital project execution.

That one principle we added to our list of "Project Alpha Team Principles" became our motivator: *78% done is better than 100% perfect.* This got recited very often - sometimes in jest, sometimes for validation, and sometimes for comfort with an uncomfortable decision. We worked through both the Thanksgiving and Christmas breaks. Work went on around the clock, with handoffs from one region to the next. As America went to sleep, Asia was waking up to continue activities.

We delivered one week ahead of what we initially referred to as a ridiculously unattainable schedule. But then, that's what we do at P&G. We solve difficult problems, even the ones with improbable risks and schedules.

God's Grace

I wholeheartedly believe I was blessed with an incredible amount of trust and favor from my colleagues working on or supporting Project Alpha, trust and empowerment from my leadership, and trust and dedication from my team. It took a high level of emotional intelligence to remain sane while I guided my team. I believe in grace, not luck. I believe in miracles, as this result gave evidence.

Leadership Principles

1. Sometimes 78% done is better than 100% perfect.
2. Have a tolerance for and deal with uncertainty proactively.
3. You will make more progress when you add data to emotions.

Chapter 14

Barrier-Buster

> **Power Scripture:**
>
> *The steps of a [good and righteous] man are directed and established by the Lord, And He delights in his way [and blesses his path].*
>
> *Psalms 37:23 (AMP)*

Problem-Solving

Leaders solve problems. This may mean leading the charge or bringing the best minds together to solve the problem. A leader's objective to problem-solving is to have the foresight to pre-empt problems by addressing situations that can evolve into problems, minimize the problems that surface, or provide leadership to solve the problems that do. It does not mean the leader must have the technical expertise necessary to solve the problem. But the leader must be a barrier-buster.

It is not logical to expect a leader to have all the answers. Surrounding yourself with empowered individuals, with the best and brightest minds, will enable you to ensure problems encountered can be addressed. As a leader, your job is to foster a culture of diligence, a bias for action to attack problems as they come, and a culture of innovation for continuous improvement. If you are solving the same problem over and over, this borders on insanity. If you expect different results while doing the same thing, you have migrated to insanity.

The leader must ensure the organization is empowered (trained, authorized, confident, and has the resources) to handle issues that arise. The leader must also ensure the problem is understood well enough to develop and implement the right solution. My situation was about ensuring my team spent sufficient time understanding the problem to get to the root cause and, as such, the right solutions.

One of my earliest assignments at P&G was to drive a new approach to the reliability of our manufacturing process. My biggest lesson from that assignment was that we tend to arrive at and settle on what we think is the problem too quickly. We would get to an assumed cause of an equipment breakdown without properly understanding the drivers and influencers to the most basic cause - the root causes. Root cause analysis is fundamental in solving technical challenges, but we seldom have the patience to work towards it. This patience was needed when my team was charged with developing a solution to a multi-million-dollar problem.

Our category was profitable, but we wanted to improve our total shareholder return and increase our global volume on one of our products. It was obvious we did not have a clear solution. The work we were doing was driving incremental improvements. I was tasked with leading a team to develop and implement a capital project that was believed to be the answer to our dilemma. Like all my previous projects, schedule was critical. I was new to that part of our business, but based on my experience, I knew how to deliver this project.

Everyone involved in that project had an idea of what the problem was and seemingly the ideal solution. And they were all different. One idea was to reapply the technology our competition was using. My response was, "If I am always following you, you will always be leading me." And I wanted us to lead. Therefore, I first had to slow my team down by leaving the laboratories and pilot plants and spending a week together developing our plan. I challenged my team that our first priority was to understand the fundamental problem we were trying to solve and ensure a strong link to our business strategy.

I pulled aside the three leaders (Tom, Jing, and Shelly) from my partner functions to form a small cross-functional core team. We focused on the business strategy, while the rest of our teams continued the improvements that were already being implemented at all of our category manufacturing plants around the globe.

My core team went into seclusion, so we could focus all our attention on the problem. We started by getting clear on the business strategy as the foundation and understanding the compelling business need. The outcome was very satisfying, and our Vice President's leadership sponsors were impressed. Next, our team needed to define the problem we wanted to solve. In a world where schedule was a convincing driver, my team agreed to spend the necessary time understanding the problem we were trying to solve by using available data and predictive models. I have a fundamental belief that very often, the problem can be defined best by those in the trenches, and, most times, they also have the solutions. Thus, I convinced my core team to travel to several of our manufacturing plants in search of their input and recommendations. We found a goldmine.

There was excitement and energy at each manufacturing plant we visited for the opportunity to work on that strategy. They defined the problem in ways we could not have predicted or guessed, yet they all pointed to similar conclusions. The data was irrefutable. The ideas for solutions were also free-flowing. In some cases, the plant managers and technicians actually generated consumer data and leveraged virtual models to demonstrate their input. Although the data they collected needed more validation, the results were directionally correct. On a few occasions, they actually built scaled-down physical models to demonstrate their points and to bring it to life. We were impressed by the technical data and depth of penetration into understanding the problem.

One thing became clear on that tour. The size of the prize was much bigger than any finance manager had previously estimated.

When we collated all the data we had collected, the information shared with us, and the ideas for solutions, our vision of the future became clearer and more exciting.

Collectively, Tom, Jing, Shelly, and I validated the principle that "if you stay with a problem long enough to understand it, the solution will present itself." And in our case, the solution became quite obvious, and of course, needed some developmental work - work we had already started but had not given much priority. The time we took to understand the problem had paid off. Led by our finance manager, our core team was able to define a size of the prize that was truly *breakthrough*.

God's Grace

When I proposed taking the time to understand the elements of the problem, I received one hundred percent support from my team and our sponsors. Everyone we interacted with was fully engaged to help define the problem. My sponsors empowered me by giving me all the resources I needed to see this through, although it was an unusual approach at that point in the project. I received strong support, and the result was welcomed. This was more confirmation of one of my favorite Bible verses: *"Do not be anxious about anything, but in everything by prayer and supplication with thanksgiving let your requests be made known unto God." Philippians 4:6 (ESV).*

Leadership Principles

1. If you stay with a problem long enough to understand it, the solution will present itself.
2. Your business strategy points to your true worth.
3. If I am always following you, you will always be leading me.

Section III
Leading with Your Head

Chapter 15

A Super Vision

Visionary

I always teased my bosses when I asked a question and they did not have the answer. I would say, "You are a supervisor. You are supposed to have a super-vision of the solution!" The reality is that vision is a foundational and basic skill for a leader to be effective.

A leader must be able to not only see the path through the forest. That leader must also see beyond the forest to the great results he or she needs to lead an organization towards or away from impending disaster.

Just having a vision is not enough. You must be able to communicate it in a way that enrolls others in adopting that vision, taking ownership of it and doing the work to get to that vision. This is where other leadership skills - like being an active listener, influencer, or communicator - become helpful.

I have seen many promising visions and ideas of a bright tomorrow fizzle and die because of poor execution. In most cases, they were sabotaged by influential members who were not aligned to the vision, and the leader did not take the time to properly enroll the organization. One underestimated critic derailed a great vision. In other cases, the vision was half-baked and not properly thought through. As such, the foundation was weak. A classic example is that of the vision and business strategy not being aligned.

Developing a vision does not only apply to the business. As a leader, it also applies to you. It is often said, "You become what you think you are." Said another way, your words can be a self-fulfilling prophecy. What you envision for yourself is what you will work towards the most. The same applies to your organization or team. They will become what you envision - if you work towards it.

After many years working in the engineering discipline at P&G, I started a new assignment in a part of the business I had never worked before. I had the responsibility of building capability across that organization throughout the world. I developed and shared my 30-day onboarding plan with my manager. This included meeting the teams in each region, assessing our current situation, and proposing a plan to move forward. My questions started flowing at the onset of my onboarding.

My first observation was that the organization was very fractured, non-standard, and non-collaborative. It was not because the organization did not want to be more productive but because there had not been a clear need to do that. This led to much brute force being used, more stress than warranted, and mismatched capability from one region to the next.

The Chinese organization had the youngest tenured group but delivered the highest productivity and almost fifty percent of the production volume for that business. The team in Latin America was a team of five that was understaffed, working out of borrowed office space, and heavily dependent on the US organization to manufacture some of their products. Everywhere I looked, I found bunches of very low-hanging fruit. To say I was needed is an understatement. After observing the myriad of opportunities, I started developing a vision of what that organization could be.

I developed a vision of what we could become, as well as the potential results in increased productivity, capability, and volume. My vision would depend on a collaborative culture with a bias for action, creativity, and innovation. I received significant tail wind when I decided to double-up on my onboarding trips by spending time providing coaching and helping the teams with their measures to track results. I also spent time actively listening to their concerns, requests for help, and ideas for improvement. I started connecting the teams across the regions so they could be more collaborative by helping one another. Together, if we worked interdependently, we could move our global mass much further than every team working independently.

The teams each had a culture that reflected the short-sightedness they were designed with. I was able to get our team leaders - who were located in Belgium, China, Venezuela, the United States, and Japan - to have regular connections where I shared a vision of what we could become. We discussed what needed to be true to make that vision come alive. They were all stressed by the work and welcomed the potential increase in capability and capacity, as well as strengthening our global culture.

My vision included renaming our organization to better reflect the work that we did. For example, instead of saying we were "Taxi Drivers" because that's what we had always been called, we would now be referred to as "Transportation Service Providers" because we had evolved to meet new requests from the business, which required us to do more than just taxi people around. The concept and recommendation were very well-received by the team and our leadership in each country.

I later brought our five team leaders together in one location for a four-day summit. The leader from China offered to host the event. This was the first time all the leaders would be together since being in their roles; one had been in his role for as long as 5 years. The key objective was to develop a plan to drive our new vision forward, and my plan was to use my organizational assessment data to redesign our organization to get the results our business demanded of us. This would include evaluating our structure, culture, communication processes, workflows, and other elements of the organizational development model. A lot had to be considered.

I designed the event so the whole Chinese organization would join us one day for an afternoon session and dinner celebration. The dinner celebration was for the outstanding results our global team was delivering and also to recognize the young Chinese team for their work. The engagement was very encouraging. The networking between the leaders was exactly what I had envisioned to foster a culture of collaboration. The team leaders and the Chinese organization were energized. By the end of the week, each leader had a plan to engage and implement what was now our new vision.

My report from the meeting would serve as the first edition of our organization's new monthly newsletter, complete with news, key results, focus on a team (the first one was the Chinese team), and special personal milestones, such as the birth of a baby, career promotions, or other special awards.

It was very uplifting to see the global organization grab hold of the vision and make it come alive. One member proposed we professionally create a logo for our organization. It could be used on letterheads, slide decks, trophies, and other items. That was a splendid idea! I launched a competition between the teams to submit proposals for our new logo. I received at least two from each team. All of our bosses voted and selected the winning proposal. Of course, the winning team was recognized with an award and bragging rights.

When I left three years later, the business results were astonishing. We had been able to deliver more innovation faster to market, which increased our production volume and profit. Our teams were cross-training each other, which built relationships and drove collaboration.

The capability of our organization had improved dramatically and was reflected in our metrics tracking defects. Our work processes had become more standardized and predictable. We had become a center of excellence for the other similar businesses within P&G.

God's Grace

I was blessed with a manager who had empowered me to drive my vision based on the gaps I saw as I connected with the regions. He expected I would help the teams learn from one another, but he did not expect that we could get to a global interdependent organization.

The other leaders allowed me to redesign their organizations to make improvements. Although they could have pushed back due to their competitive spirits or been blinded by their business pressures, getting them to talk to each other, to stop for a week to develop an action plan and to connect with their teams directly led to them granting me the favor needed to make my vision come to life.

Leadership Principles

1. If you don't have a vision of where you want to go, any road will take you there.
2. Poor leaders drive dependency. Good leaders drive independency. Great leaders drive interdependency that exceeds expectations.
3. Your vision only comes alive when it is adopted and owned by your organization.

Chapter 16

Mountain-Mover

Influence

Influence is a critical skill of great leaders. It is your ability to impact others' behaviors, actions, and choices. This is on full display through social influence. One great social influencer in sports or music who wears a new outfit can influence a whole nation to run out and buy that outfit in a matter of hours after it is seen on social media!

In the business world, a leader who is respected, who has high integrity and can be trusted, is very influential. That influence is what allows a leader to sell a vision, engage others in that vision, and motivate them to move towards that vision. It is what allows the leader to gain loyal followers without unhealthy persuasion, threats, or peer pressure. People want to follow influential leaders.

Being influential does not mean you are a great person. There are many influencers who lead others in the wrong direction by encouraging them to make poor choices, often in the best interest of the influencer or just because they can.

As a leader, your words and actions matter. You are being watched and emulated by your admirers and followers. Being a great leader with influence means adding the human element to your leadership tool box. This includes empathy and leading with the heart to care for others.

While I was new to the job in my situation below, I was blessed with strong sponsorship, which allowed me to influence the leaders I needed, so that I could change course on our process technology.

Two-thirds of the way through my career at P&G, I wanted an assignment that was totally different from what I had done in the past. Therefore, I started a new assignment in a new sector of our company. There was a need to improve our technology platform to be more standardized, agile, and productive. The key need was driving cost down. It was a great aspiration, but when the masses are heading down one path, it becomes hard for a newcomer to change the direction, even though it is based on data. What do you do when emotions are high but the direction you are heading in does not support the business' compelling needs? That was the question I asked myself when faced with that situation.

I came into the assignment with much global experience driving platforms that delivered high productivity, that were game-changers and breakthrough technologies. Now, as I journeyed through the assessment phase of my onboarding, I became very aware of the prevailing thoughts driving the choices being made. Generally, they were based on "sustaining ideas" versus "breakthrough ideas." These would not get our business in a global leadership position. The competition was not sitting still, but instead of working on an innovative solution, our lead idea was to use the same equipment technologies that our competition was using at that time.

Following my accelerated onboarding, I pulled my team together to share my observations and get their input on the direction we should take. I always believe the answers are on the shop floor. And sure enough, although my team was following the directions of their previous leader, they had their own passionate thoughts on the path we should have been following.

I challenged them to start from a blank sheet and help me capture the vision of where we should be heading. Nothing was off the table. Some ideas were status quo; others were bold and radical. I then spent some time receiving their feedback on the current approach. It was painfully obvious they had a lot of input, but it did not appear their concerns and ideas were being considered.

The group provided more data and input than I was led to believe existed by those who were driving down the current path. The team members behaved as if they were in a new sandbox. They were building off each other's ideas. It was like the team was free to create.

The data they provided validated my view of our current status - slow to respond and expensive to change.

I was able to reach the team on their level and pull out the data, which supported the path we should be taking. We ended a very successful period by drafting the communication plan to our leadership. It captured an assessment of our current status, the basis for change, and reason to believe in the change.

Working with the key stakeholders and influencers, I was able to translate our technical challenges into soundbites our leaders could understand. I also detailed linkages to the top and bottom line. This enabled me to develop and share a plan that supported the business need and was in alignment with the direction our senior leaders wanted to take us. They were excited to see some real data that supported our position. I did not have a solution, but I had a plan to get us there. However, my plan needed middle management's support. It was not enough to have upper leadership's support. We needed to convince our bosses this was the right thing to do.

Based on the family culture of that business, I designed a townhall style working session for middle management. It was to share our discoveries and to provide them an opportunity to share their perspectives. Although I had a vision of the path ahead, it was imperative to get their input, buy-in, and support. They were the experts. Some of them had been in this business all their careers. I was not an expert, but I knew I could help them get to the destination.

I emailed a well-thought-out invitation to the middle managers and copied my sponsors. Because I was new to the team, I asked my sponsors (to whom the middle managers reported) to each add a supporting comment to my emailed invitation. This provided encouragement for the middle managers to make this event a priority. I followed up with the key program owners who were leading the charge on the current direction. The intent was to clarify that the meeting was not to define a path forward but to understand the current situation and gain some perspective on the direction based on new data.

I set up the townhall to be more like a working session. I even had the conference room set up with round banquet tables to facilitate small group discussions. The event was focused on cost, competition, organizational capability, and culture. New data was provided that had been available but not leveraged and, in some cases, provided new information for questions that had never been asked but should have been considered. I encouraged full interactivity with the disclaimer that, as everyone may have known, I was not the expert in that business and that although I had a nice slide presentation, I had more questions than answers. While I facilitated the event, I enlisted my team to lead various sections of the presentation.

The first part of the presentation drew some polite debate. Sensing this could get more contentious and discourage folks from listening with an open mind, I shared a ground principle I wanted us to follow. If someone had a differing point of view, that person needed to make a request or a recommendation, rather than beginning a debate. The act of trying to turn a negative position into a request or recommendation took much of the sting out of the disagreements and made the conversations more forward-focused.

Coupled with the grounding principle, the data my team shared was compelling. The section on the competition grabbed everyone's attention. I sensed when the atmosphere shifted from defensive to collaborative. I allowed others to take the lead in the discussion as they felt the need, contributing their own data or personal experiences. The finance manager, for example, who was not on my team, took over and made a passionate plea for a step change in driving cost down further than where we were trending. It was not long before the energy of the room changed to problem definition and idea generation. It was great to see the organization of leaders, across functions, engaged in an exercise that was defining our path forward. To solidify the experience, I asked at the end for members to share what excited them the most about the event we'd just had. The responses reminded me that God always comes through for me. It also reminded me why I loved that great company.

God's Grace

Grace is defined as unmerited favor. That organization, from my team members to my leadership, allowed me to influence them in a way that delivered excellence and productivity for our business. There was some pushback from those who had been working on this for a while. However, as they saw the data, they were willing to listen with open minds.

Leadership Principles

1. Always seek first to understand.
2. Leadership influence increases as trust increases.
3. Mastery earns you the right to be able to influence.

Chapter 17

It's Not Personal

> **Power Scripture:**
>
> *For God did not give us a spirit of timidity or cowardice or fear, but [He has given us a spirit] of power and of love and of sound judgement and personal discipline [abilities that result in a calm, well-balanced mind and self-control].*
>
> *2 Timothy 1:7 (AMP)*

Emotional Intelligence

The job of a leader can be stressful and taxing. Competition is constantly increasing and success more fleeting. The demands placed on us sometimes strain our emotions. As a professional, we are expected to remain even keel in the fire, no matter how personal it may seem.

Emotional intelligence is our ability to understand, manage, and take control of our own emotions and to be aware of and handle the emotions and feelings of others. It allows us to not only manage our emotions but also use good judgement and empathy when dealing with interpersonal relationships.

Why is emotional intelligence important? It allows us to reduce stress and not take on negative energy. It enables us to communicate more effectively, especially in the middle of an emotional fire when we may need to defuse conflict. We are better able to handle criticism and take accountability without passing blame or giving excuses. Someone with a high level of emotional intelligence will quickly apologize when wrong and move on. Their self-confidence is not shattered by a miss. Emotional intelligence gives us the ability to better empathize with others and understand their feelings and frames of reference. This allows us to be in the present and actively listening when facing someone who needs empathy.

The bottom line is that having a strong level of emotional intelligence will help you remain as stress-free as possible and not take every challenging interaction personal - even if sometimes they are, as in my situation below.

I was nearing the end of my career at P&G, and although I was always loaded with work, it was normal for my manager, Martha, to ask me to help with a particular challenge in another part of the company. Therefore, I was not surprised when she asked me to use my skills to help in another business category that was under her leadership. She knew that I was already in a role that had me swamped and in the middle of a project execution that needed a miracle to implement. However, she asked me to help out because none of the leaders on that project had the collaboration skills that were needed for its success. And failure of that project was not an option.

Martha asked if I could free up ten percent of my time and devote it to that project. I quickly worked with my team to put the lower-priority issues on the back burner, re-negotiated some commitments, and delegated some of my tasks. That freed up about twenty percent of my time, which I thought would be sufficient based on my experience. The time needed is always double the time sold to me.

I quickly identified the problem during my onboarding for the new project. One of my peers, Jack, who held a critical lead role on the project, was proving to be a stumbling block, masquerading as a gatekeeper. To make it worse, he demonstrated characteristics of a bully. Several women and minority managers had issues with his style and approach to them. He was very influential with leadership, and feedback only seemed to have been met with passive retaliation. As a minority, it was not long before I became his next target, which I attributed to him feeling threatened by me.

During my first conference call with the new team to share my plan of action, he publicly shut down every proposal for improvement that I presented. I'm used to critique. What was different was his approach and gloveless punches towards me as a (new) team member. Knowing his history and being surprised by his behavior as a key leader, I chose to listen but mentally filed away his critique, which was opinionated and had no merit. I did that by practicing the following scripture: "*Understand this, my beloved brothers and sisters. Let everyone be quick to hear [be a careful, thoughtful listener], slow to speak [a speaker of carefully chosen words and], slow to anger [patient, reflective, forgiving]." James 1:19–20 (AMP).*

Following the meeting, I called the needed team members to initiate the implementation of my plan based on their input. Later that day, I stopped by Jack's office. I wanted to understand why he'd felt the need to personally attack me in front of the team, considering that we had completed what I thought was an effective join-up and that he knew I was only there to help. I already knew how Jack felt about me, so it was a long shot, but I was hoping we could work through our differences, or at least agree on a civil approach to working together. However, Jack quickly validated what I already knew.

"Hey, Jack," I announced my approach as I got closer to his cubicle.

"Good afternoon, Kennedy," Jack replied.

"Dude, are you doing OK? You left me a little worried about you. So, I wanted to check on you to see if all is well, considering your reactions on the call this morning. I wanted to understand what happened this morning and how I can help."

"Kennedy, to be frank, I think that is the problem. There is nothing you can do to help."

"Oh. I am sorry you feel that way. But are we talking about me helping you or helping the project?" I responded.

"I do not see a need for you to be on this project. You have never worked in this category. The technology is unique, and I don't believe you have any additional skills, nor can you offer anything new that I have not experienced in my many years working in this category." Jack then drew the line by continuing, "Martha (who was also his boss) ordered me to work with you, so I will try to do just that, but don't expect any warm fuzzies from me." The furrows between Jack's eyebrows were rather deep from his stress.

I clearly remember thinking to myself while Jack was talking, *Oh, boy, I was brought here not just to help this project, but this was for me to strengthen my emotional intelligence, and this poor guy is my test subject. I am so sorry for him.*

Jack continued to speak very openly. So, instead of me getting angry, debating, or walking out, I spent some time asking Jack questions to further understand his mindset. I did more listening and observing the energy lost in his stonewalling. The discussion did not go well - for him. He was angry. I was not. I made a personal declaration to treat his resistance as a positive force to help my personal development and to deliver a more quality product to the business.

"Jack, you know what?"

"What?" Jack fired back.

"I really do want to thank you for sharing your open and honest feelings," I said as I turned to leave when I had enough information. "I did not realize you felt the way you do. I hope over time you will see the value I bring." I had confirmed to myself that this was personal. The best course of action at that point was for me to walk away. I chose not to invest my emotions in this man and did not take it as a personal attack. I did not have an issue. He did. Besides, I really had too much to do. This also made it easier for me to manage and control my emotions.

Jack's attack on my work continued for a couple weeks during meetings and via email exchanges. Juggling two jobs and receiving a lot of support and alignment from the rest of this new team (except Jack), I kept moving forward, but I could not let it go on. I was concerned about the impact that Jack's dysfunctional behavior was having on the rest of the team.

On several occasions, he would respond negatively to my emails, copying our entire team. He would typically begin his response with, "Kennedy, I request that you stop because this is not helpful," or, "Kennedy, you're creating confusion in the organization." One evening, while working late, I received one of those emails. I decided to respond, not to lash out, but to provide a controlled response to help the team understand they needed to stay the course and not be distracted by Jack's push.

I started by thanking him for keeping the team entertained and declaring that it was a badge of honor to be seen by him as not being helpful and not conforming to his tactics. I also wrote that it meant I was doing something different, which is what the project needed. I acknowledged I heard him, and for now, my focus was on driving the project's success. I also wrote that I would love for him and me to discuss his concerns post startup over coffee at my expense. I closed by sharing that the company had a very effective escalation process, which I encouraged him to use, if that would bring him relief from the stress he was under. However, I requested he direct his energy to delivering the project's objectives, or I could help him with other choices *(in case you are wondering, yes, I did close with that offer - not a threat).* I thoroughly enjoyed writing my response. When I was done, I touched - but did not hit - the "Send" button on my computer.

I was very tired. So, just in case I was reacting from stress or anger, I decided to practice what I normally coach my mentees to do: document the response, then sleep on it for twenty-four hours. That was actually harder to do than my coaching. The next day, I evaluated whether or not it was a wise decision and whether the wording reflected what I wanted to communicate not only to Jack but also to the team without giving up my power by reacting angrily. So, I made some minor changes. *Send.*

Two things happened after I sent the email. First, I received a private "Thank You" email, phone call, or instant message from virtually each of the members. Second, I never received another nasty response to my emails from Jack again. Unfortunately, he continued to demonstrate he did not want me on the project, but his pushback and critiques were more tempered, controlled, and professional.

I eventually had a conversation with Martha with an understanding that she would not intervene but allow me to work through the situation with Jack. I needed to understand her perspective on his actions towards me. She shared that he was upset due to a boundary I had set before accepting her help request. My boundary was that I would not report to him based on my principle that it is never helpful for a peer to report to another peer. Plus, my background data on him was filled with examples of his unhealthy relationships with respect to minorities. My boundary was not shared with him, but his request to maintain full leadership and for me to receive direction from him was denied. He was not happy. Having that understanding, I was able to help maneuver a more collaborative relationship between Jack and myself. I took him out to lunch one day, and we had a great conversation on feedback and styles. I offered to partner with him to continue discussing personal styles over coffee, if he so chose. He accepted. I was shocked.

Before leaving the restaurant, I said, "I would appreciate if you give me feedback like cereal. I will enjoy it better in a bowl, rather than pouring it on my head." He laughed. I continued, "And I suspect other people would appreciate it that way also."

"Point taken," Jack responded.

God's Grace

God gave me the emotional intelligence to handle Jack's attacks. This helped me execute the plan that was ahead of me. It also helped me stand my ground and make wise and strategic choices, which helped me provide leadership to the team. God also gave me so much favor with Jack's team that some of them actually wanted to petition me replacing him. They gave me critical information, which helped me navigate the pond in which I was swimming with this shark. I would not have been successful in this job if it had not been for God's Grace and for His help in keeping my emotions under control as I navigated my responses.

Leadership Points

1. If you are a leader and no one is following, you are just out for a walk.
2. Treat resistance as a positive force.
3. Leaders give feedback like cereal, in a bowl to be useful, versus poured over the head.

Chapter 18

What Matters Most

Power Scripture:

But seek first his kingdom and his righteousness, and all these things will be given to you as well.

Matthew 6:33 (NIV)

Priority-Setting

I know of no leader who does not have more to do than time allows. There is a constant need to address multiple and, often, competing priorities at the same time. Being able to prioritize is not enough. You need to be able to set the *right* priorities.

There are some situations that demand immediate attention but may be of lower priority, like a ringing phone. Although the ringer may sound urgent - and most of us will drop everything to answer the phone - that may not be the case. There have been many times I dropped something important that I was doing to answer the phone only to find a scammer on the other end.

Of course, what is of high priority to you may not be a priority at all to me. As a leader, it is important to be clear on priorities. This enables your organization to make better choices and avoid missing your expectations.

You cannot lead effectively if you can't set priorities. There's no way around that. However, how good are you at balancing competing home and work priorities? There is a good chance that if you struggle with balancing work/home priorities you will not be able to empathize, understand, or coach your direct reports with similar challenges. One of my managers brought me face to face with that understanding early in my career.

We can get so wrapped up in our corporate jobs that we miss out on the important things in life, or worse, forget about them altogether and relegate them to a far lower priority than delivering our business results. This is one area that was not difficult for me when I started; I imagine that is the case for most young professionals. My priorities were clear, and I would not compromise. Of course, that was before I met Leroy, and my commitment got its first real test on priorities in my professional life.

At the beginning of my career with P&G, I was a process engineer traveling weekly to one of our manufacturing plants for a very important capital project to support a new product. We knew the competition was trying to make a similar product. The industry competition was fierce. We were all doing everything possible to get to market first.

I was the startup leader who was also responsible for the liquid and dry powder material handling systems of some of our product's key ingredients. I was working some very long hours with my team. When we progressed to startup, my team and I took up temporary residence at the installation site. We rented corporate housing, which was much better than a hotel room and much more cost-effective. We would return home every two weeks on a Friday evening for a weekend, then back to the site by noon on Monday. Work at the site was hectic. Our days were long. We would be exhausted from walking from one end of the plant to the next and up ten stories to where the dry chemicals were stored.

One morning, I was paged on the plant's intercom to come to the control room for a phone call from my home office. That was unusual. Normally, the person would leave a message, and I would call back at a break. Paging me on the plant's intercom would receive a quicker response. "It must be serious," I thought, so I briskly made my way to the control room. I took up the phone receiver, and my home office administrative assistant, Sandy, was on the other end.

"Hello? This is Kennedy Germain."

"Kennedy. This is Sandy," the voice came back.

"Hi Sandy," I said. "Is everything okay?" I almost did not want to hear the response.

"No, Kennedy," she said. "Your wife fell down your stairs from the second floor to the first floor at your house. I called your brother to take her to the hospital. I also called her doctor to let him know she was hurt and on her way to his office."

"Jesus!" I said, the only one-word prayer I could think of. I felt the blood drain from my face, my stomach twisting into a knot. My knees went weak.

I don't recall my reaction after that. But I do remember the control room becoming very silent, except for an electronic alarm going "beep – beep – beep – beep" on one of the consoles. I could hear the perpetual hum of the running process operation as it persisted, as if providing a soothing white noise to my disturbed spirit and anxious soul. And I was seated. Not sure when I took the seat. The team, in the control room, had followed the conversation from my responses. What the whole team knew was that my wife was six months pregnant. She needed me now, and I was more than six hundred miles away from her.

"Thank you, Sandy," I said. "I am on my way back to Cincinnati." I knew every flight back to Cincinnati from our location and that there was one leaving in a couple hours. I asked her to book me on that flight.

I shared the news with the team members who were in the control room. Everyone rallied behind me to get home quickly. Someone offered to drive me to the airport. Another quickly proposed a plan to have my responsibilities covered while I was out. We had developed a great backup plan in 5 minutes. The last step was just to share the news and plan with my project manager. My direct manager was in Cincinnati, but while on site, the project manager, Leroy, was responsible for me and the rest of the engineering team.

Leroy listened attentively . . . too attentively . . . while I was clearly frantic.

He then casually said, "Well, Kennedy, because your brother is taking your wife to the doctor, I should think you should be able to stay here and go home on Friday as planned." It was Wednesday.

"Leroy, my wife is six months pregnant," I reminded him. "And she just went bumpety bump all the way down the stairs, and you want me to stay here for another two days?" I could feel my emotions welling up inside of me, and I was about to explode. My hands were shaking.

He calmly replied, "Yes. We are at a critical point in the project where we are testing one of your temperature-monitoring inventions, and you need to be here for it."

"And I will be here for it," I interrupted. "The team created a plan to delay my test and pull up another operation in my absence."

"Sorry, but I cannot approve your trip back today."

At that point, I was faced with the inevitable. I had to choose my priority. I suddenly felt a boldness rise up in me. It was an easy decision, and I was at peace. I got up and said, "Sorry, Leroy, but I need to go take care of my pregnant wife and eighteen-month-old son. We can discuss anything you want when I return next week."

With that, I marched out of Leroy's office to begin my long-and-way-too-slow journey back to Cincinnati. I prayed all the way to my corporate apartment, where I grabbed my suitcase and continued all the way to the airport, asking God for His protection and mercy. I called my boss in Cincinnati from a phone in the airport to update him on what had transpired. Sandy had already informed him. He supported my decision.

God's Grace

I experienced God's Grace through my administrative assistant, who had been able to handle the situation for me by mobilizing my brother, contacting my wife's doctor, and setting up my flight. I still can't understand how she was able to pull all these pieces together so quickly. I also experienced God's Grace through my teammates and colleagues at the plant, who had been able to cover for me, had kept us on schedule, and had supported my trip home. They were probably part of the reason I still had a job when I returned.

Leadership Principles

1. Win with what really matters.
2. Be very clear on personal priorities.
3. Take care of your employees, and they will take care of your results.

Chapter 19

Unapologetically Confident

> **Power Scripture:**
>
> *If any of you lacks wisdom, [to guide him through a decision or circumstance], he is to ask of [our benevolent] God, who gives to everyone generously and without rebuke or blame, and it will be given to him.*
>
> *James 1:5 (AMP)*

Self-Confidence

Self-confidence is not the same as being full of pride or arrogance. To be prideful or arrogant is to assume you are entitled. Self-confidence, on the other hand, is being sure of your ability and competency to deliver. It means trusting yourself to get the job done.

A leader who does not have self-confidence will find it difficult to inspire and influence others - a core outcome of leadership. Lacking self-confidence will result in your capability being eroded, being unsteady in your judgement, and wavering in your decisions. You will also be easily influenced to go against your better judgement.

Self-confident leaders are not on an ego trip, do not have a need to bully others, and do not spend time trying to prove their capabilities to critics. Instead of feeling "entitled," self-confident leaders tend to feel blessed and are not threatened by others.

Self-confident leaders have an *abundance mentality* (versus a *scarcity mentality*). They are self-motivated and do not look for the approval of others to motivate them. Therefore, they are very comfortable practicing shared leadership and allowing others to take the lead in areas of their expertise, as needed. Self-confident leaders also have a strong focus on empowering others to be successful. Concerning decision-making, acknowledging when wrong comes easy to self-confident leaders.

Self-confident leaders demonstrate a high level of emotional intelligence. They do not let others' emotional instability cause them undue stress, as demonstrated in my situation below.

There is a particular work process we used at P&G that would deliver the right answer to particular questions being asked about a supply chain. This does not mean the answers you get are the ones you wanted or expected. However, any supply chain can be designed properly, depending on the outcomes you need from it. Midway through my career, I became one of the company experts who spent years teaching that process and creating solutions around the globe.

Based on my experience, I was brought into a project as a technical expert to help solve a critical business gap in a supply chain in Venezuela. We needed a fast solution. Julian, the General Manager for Latin America, was confident that a proper solution was needed.

I began by creating an execution plan. I then scheduled a meeting to present the plan to Johnathan, one of the leaders on the team. My intent was to get his input on the plan of execution, considering he was a student of the work process. Johnathan brought Jorge to the meeting. Jorge was another leader who had responsibility for part of the product we were working on. I started by sharing a short flow chart of my implementation plan. I started to get into the specifics, when Johnathan interrupted.

"Your plan is too elaborate and complex for what we need," he said.

"And the answer was already obvious," Jorge interjected, as he voiced support for Johnathan's position.

I thought to myself, *If the answer was so obvious, why is the supply chain so messed up?*

Feedback is a gift and should be given in a way that is useful. Criticism is part of the landscape of any leader. If you receive no criticism and everyone always agrees with your approach, then you may be a conformist and not really leading. Knowing that helped me stay focused rather than internalizing every disagreement.

"Thanks for the feedback. Would you guys give me the opportunity to finish sharing what I have? Then we can discuss it?" I asked.

The detailed plan only gave them more food for rebuttal. I suggested to Johnathan and Jorge that, before jumping to a conclusion, they allow me one month to connect with Julian and his leadership team to help me understand his region's needs. I already had a trip scheduled for Caracas, Venezuela, and the timing was perfect. This would at least tell us if we were on the right track.

"No!" Johnathan responded emphatically. "Won't happen because Julian is new and really does not understand his market yet." I couldn't recall the last time a manager's "no" response had been so emphatic. I'd had to calm myself by counting down from ten and taking a couple of deep breaths.

"Don't you believe that, as the leader of that region, Julian would be in the best position to speak for his business?" I challenged Johnathan but was only met with more resistance from both individuals. They ignored my plan and proceeded to lecture me on what I was going to do and the process Johnathan requested that I follow. Johnathan then went to the whiteboard and mapped out the plan. There was one problem. The process they shared with me was fundamentally flawed and incorrect. I was surprised because this work process was a core skill needed for Johnathan's job. He should have known it well enough to teach it. That clearly was not the case. That actually brought a calm to my spirit. Jonathan now appeared as a Biblical Goliath to be knocked down with five small stones. His bark had no bite. His stinger was not painful. He needed my help.

When they were done, I took another deep breath, stood up, and proceeded with an unapologetic, deeply passionate, and as controlled as possible response. Sometimes, I even squeezed out a smile. I explained that Johnathan should have known I was an expert in this workflow and that I was surprised he did not realize the process he had just shared was incorrect. I indicated three fundamental flaws in the process he outlined. I reminded him that I had been asked to help his team. I suggested he reconnect with his Vice President about his concerns and, if aligned, determine their path forward. I also suggested that they get expert help to uncover the answers they needed. I concluded by sharing that I knew my capability and debating it with them was not in my best interest, as it would not move the business forward. I turned to leave. Jorge stopped me.

At that point, they dropped the drama and apologized. Johnathan said, "I'm just concerned about some 'hot-shot' coming here thinking they have all the answers when we have been working on this for a while. We both want to be part of the process and provide our input."

I sat down and responded, "Apology accepted. Thank you for thinking I'm a 'hot-shot.' I'm really just confident in my capability and know I can help the team with this work process, but only if you support it. And, of course you will have input. As you know, the first step in the process is gathering leadership expectations. If you had allowed me to share my slides, you would have seen your names on the list of leaders I intended to interview. I also look to you to help with facilitation. I can provide a refresher if desired."

This was only one of the many times my skills and capabilities were either taken for granted or aggressively challenged. I was confident in the capabilities I had been blessed with and was always happy to share them to help drive the business forward, if warranted. However, although I was always willing to share my capabilities if needed for understanding, I never saw a need to debate them - especially when the motivation was biased.

God's Grace

Over the years, God has opened doors of favor to me, which has led to me having a toolbox of unique skills. These skills have enabled me to contribute to my company in areas that others would not have expected. In this case, one of my sponsors had reached out to me several years before and encouraged me to develop that skill, which helped me navigate many challenges and barriers from those who wanted a quick answer from that work process.

Leadership Principles

1. It is more important to understand rather than shoot down an idea because it is not aligned with yours.
2. Do not confuse arrogance with self-confidence. Self-confidence is empowering. Arrogance is alienating.
3. Self-confident leaders do not let others' emotional instability cause them undue stress.

Chapter 20

Speak Up

Power Scripture:

Be gracious in your speech. The goal is to bring out the best in others in a conversation, not put them down, not cut them out.

Colossians 4:6 (MSG)

Communication

There are leaders who talk a lot but seldom communicate. Communication is more than you talking at others. If you are talking and no one is listening, you are just engaging in a linguistic exercise. As a leader, good communication skills are important because they allow you to transfer the right information, to the right people, in the right format, with the right heart, so they can hear and be inspired by you, and most importantly, so you can hear them. It gives you the ability to transfer information up to management and to every level in a way that is received.

Good communicators also take the time to listen when others are not in alignment, have concerns, or have difficulty with the message being communicated. My situation below required active listening and being able to share unwanted data so that the best decision could be made.

I believe in the eventual outcome when a well-designed work process with a proven track record is followed. Work processes drive efficiency and predictability. They provide data to drive the right decisions. Sometimes we may not like the outcome we are being directed towards, so we question the process. Forget the fact that we loved it when it gave us the outcome we wanted! Sometimes, questioning the process is right, especially when it's based on understanding and continuous improvement. However, often when we question the process, it is because we have a solution in search of a problem, and we are heading down the wrong path. We should begin with a well-defined problem in search of a solution. When we follow the work process and the outcome is not what we want, it becomes easier to make the resulting decision because we know we used the best available data, just like my business leader had to do for one of my projects.

My organization was driving an exceptionally large capital project to relaunch one of our products. We had been working on it for a couple years, but there were significant challenges to overcome. One was the cost; another was a proposition that would win the consumer's heart. It was a great initiative with awesome technology in its formulation and packaging. It was also giving us the opportunity to install some manufacturing capabilities that would reduce our manufacturing cost of capacity. This was a global project with input from all relevant regions. I was not only the engineering lead on the project but also an expert for a work process we could use to drive the integrated business strategy on that project. I knew that this work process would drive the best decision, but because it was new, it was not as widely used as it should have been. It required discipline and diligence.

At one of our leadership team meetings, I provided clear data and information and recommended that we leverage that particular work process. It was agreed that this project was complex enough and large enough in scope to make this an ideal application. It had to be applied to each region we were impacting, and that required input from the general managers (GMs) with responsibility for their regional business strategies.

As expected, I quickly received many strong suggestions from a few of the members on our team to take shortcuts or make modifications to the process so that our schedule would not be impacted. Of course, for every suggestion to modify the process, I had an example of the potential subsequent poor results. Anything worth doing is worth doing right. I subscribe to the principle that you should never settle for mediocrity in the name of efficiency.

I took the time to listen to their concerns and proposals. I then engaged in a conversation to understand the background of their concerns. I also actively listened to understand if those were truly data-driven concerns, a political stunt, or simply unjustified fear. If it was a stunt, then our conversation would just be a linguistic exercise, and I would not be communicating. Generally, their concerns were from lack of understanding. Therefore, I scheduled a separate meeting where I took the time to share and demonstrate when and how each of their valid concerns would be addressed through the work process. Taking the time to actively listen to them versus brushing them aside proved even more beneficial. As an outcome of the meeting, together we strengthened some less-than-solid areas of the execution plan and created an exit plan in the event that the process got bogged down in morass. This, on one hand, gave comfort to the critics that they were being heard, and, on the other hand, increased interest in the others to learn more about that work process.

Fortunately, my work and approach were well-respected, valued, and appreciated by all our regional GMs. This paved the way for the regional core teams to work collaboratively with me. My communication with each regional team was tailored to their specific situation. The result was a faster integration of all inputs and less swirl around the process. As the regional teams felt as if they were a part of the process, they became more open to engage in the work process and shared improvement suggestions, as well as provided added data to strengthen the analysis.

The process highlighted something we already knew from volumes of consumer data but that was not truly integrated into this project at that point: the different needs and wants of consumers in different markets. It forced the tough conversations we were glossing over due to speed and drove out the assumptions we were making. The process kept the overarching business needs in front of us and drove the linkages, if any, between the business strategy and the design concepts of our project.

The work progressed well and started bringing into focus a painful fact: our design concept would not meet the needs in all the regions in scope. The data suggested that our standard global design should instead be regionalized. This was a radical change from the direction of the project. I had to share the outcome with my global lead team and the recommendation to stop, or redefine, the project's strategic direction. My business leader and program manager both thanked me for the courage to share what they did not want to hear, but they understood the work process and its business advantage.

God's Grace

I believe my projects were blessed by the Grace of God through me. This was one example in which we could have invested a lot more funds without realizing the assumed returns. God gave me favor with the lead team, who was aligned with my recommendation. He also gave the GMs trust and respect for me and support for the new direction.

Leadership Principles

1. Never settle for mediocrity in the name of efficiency.
2. Anything worth doing is worth doing right.
3. If you are talking and no one is listening, you're just engaging in a linguistic exercise.

Chapter 21

No Dead Bodies

| **Power Scripture:**

A soft and gentle and thoughtful answer turns away wrath, But harsh and painful and careless words stir up anger.

Proverbs 15:1 (AMP)

Conflict

Leaders tend to operate in a world of constant stress. This is especially true where you have a bias for action or are driving significant change. And as long as we are human, stress will sometimes create conflict. A leader must have a strong emotional intelligence to manage conflict when it comes. And it is not always easy to resolve.

Recognize that every situation is different. Therefore, using situational leadership will help determine how to approach and manage the conflict, versus responding the same way to everyone or every situation or expecting a happy resolution each time. As a leader, managing conflict means staying focused and choosing your battles.

Knowing that people choose how cooperative and collaborative they want to be, not every conflict is worth the effort needed to get to an agreeable end point. And not every conflict will be resolved in an agreeable position. Ending the ones that can't be resolved is sometimes in the best interest of all parties. Sometimes, the best course of action is just to forgive other people's hurtful behaviors so that you can be at peace and move on.

Managing conflict, as a leader, means knowing when to drive for a peaceful resolution, which could come in the form of solving the misunderstanding, negotiating a peaceful agreement, or even agreeing to disagree via a handshake. There are times when the resolution is not so warm at heart and forgiveness is needed. Know when to walk away if the conflict can't be resolved.

Your ability to manage and resolve conflict well reduces your stress level and ensures that you lead your organization in a controlled manner. It will also go well toward an agreeable solution, and you will gain trust and respect in the process, as in my situation below.

Towards the end of my career with P&G, I joined a project where we were in collaboration with another company, shipping one of our products to new markets. The results were phenomenal. Both companies were experiencing unprecedented growth and profit in that venture. As expected, the supply system was not optimized for this new expansion. It was taking all of our creativity to deliver our product to our customers. The agility and creativity of the team were nothing short of remarkable. We did what had to be done and literally brute-forced product through the supply chain with lots of phone calls and many late nights tracking shipments - sometimes driving to ports to confirm a shipment had made it before the dock cutoff time. There were frequent touches, frequent meetings, many passionate phone calls, numerous flaming email messages, and countless corrections and modifications. It was a war zone. Our team looked like battered and bloodied soldiers committed to winning a war. Every successful shipment was counted towards our success criteria.

Although we were getting the work done, the process to deliver our product was not sustainable. It was also negatively impacting relationships of the teams across both companies. It was my responsibility to eliminate barriers and ensure the supply system was optimized.

We had a process to design and optimize the supply systems in our company. It was amazingly effective in identifying gaps. Based on my evaluation of the issues we dealt with daily across the globe, I knew the optimization process would help.

I presented the recommendation to our leadership team. There was initial pushback due to fear that we would overburden the system with corporate red tape and kill the agility of the supply system. No one wanted to sacrifice agility for efficiency. Fortunately, I was able to explain the process in a way that eliminated or reduced the fear.

What makes a process work is involving the key stakeholders, particularly those who have data, history, and technical understanding. Thus, this initiative required all the key players from the different regions to come together for a week-long exercise, which would start at one of our suppliers and culminate at the manufacturing plant where the product was being made. This exercise required the whole team to start together, work through the exercises together, and end together. The planning was going like a well-oiled machine. There was cautious excitement among the team. I was moving at lightning speed to implement this plan. The health of our team culture needed it.

Our results were great but precariously depended on our aggressive drive and *MacGyver*-ing of solutions to problems we found. All the pieces of my plan needed to address and fix the problem were falling into place. Then, wham! I ran into a massive roadblock that was more like a retaining wall. Firm. Unmovable. Unexpected. Actually, from the *last* place I would expect: the leader of the manufacturing plant, Alfred. A quick check proved he had taken a position that was challenging for progress. I had a choice. I chose the high road. I had work to do. After all, my Bible says, *"If possible, as far as it depends on you, live at peace with everyone." Romans 12:18 (AMP).*

My first inclination was to choose not to take his pushback as personal and to seek first to understand what appeared to be an irrational position. I needed to understand whether I should escalate this issue quickly to our leader or whether we could work through it effectively. I knew Alfred to be a strong leader, so I was confused. But *conflict shows true character.*

After a number of conversations, I was able to see Alfred's motivation. He was passionately against the collaborative effort with the other company and did not see it as being good for our side of the business. Our discussions transformed into negotiations. I offered to cover the travel expenses of his employees, who were critical to the work process optimization effort, so it would not affect his plant's budget. I knew he was doing what he thought was right. I also knew he was not the ultimate approver of the initiative.

Time was not on our side to get to our comfort zone. I did not have the time to keep playing ping-pong with our conversations. He would request information; I would provide it. I would ask for his concerns, he would share an excuse. A decision was needed quickly. Therefore, following our second conversation, I shared with him my next steps for his understanding (not approval). First, I would provide the data to him to support the basis for my recommendation to optimize the supply chain (as if he did not know). If that did not meet his needs, I would escalate the decision to our sponsor.

Alfred confidently suggested that escalating for a rapid decision was best because he was under a lot of pressure. He thoroughly expected his manager to support his position. He shared transparently that my request was the lowest on his priority list. I realized my colleague was overwhelmed and was therefore *blinded by his business pressures*. In my role, I had a broader view of that part of the business than he did, as well as a better understanding of the criticality of optimizing that supply system. It was too important to our success to do otherwise.

As process owner, I escalated the issue to our business leader. As I expected, the direction given was to proceed with my plan and for Alfred to assign my requested participants from his organization to support the exercise. Alfred agreed to proceed but offered ways to accelerate and streamline the process by reducing the steps. That was not an option. My position was that although I wanted *progress over perfection, I would not settle for mediocrity in the name of efficiency*.

One week before the exercise was to begin, Alfred called me to thank me for working through the situation with him. He said he respected my job and understood why this was important. However, the pressures he was dealing with and what he had to balance did not allow him the luxury to just drop and support the collaboration. He had nothing against me. I conveyed that I understood his stress and did not take his pushback as being personal. In fact, I tried to help by offering to cover the travel expenses for his employees during the exercise, which he accepted.

The exercise far exceeded my expectations. Not only was the process optimized, but we also uncovered some simple miscommunications due to language and cultural differences. By far, the greatest success was to see the relationships that were strengthened amongst the team and true partnerships formed as a result of spending time together.

God's Grace

One of my mentors used to say, "Freedom comes with excellence." My excellent results allowed my leaders to empower me to do what was needed to drive the business. I did not take their support for this initiative lightly. Although Alfred objected to the exercise, God gave me favor with his employees, who saw the value of what I was trying to do. In the end, they were able to creatively eliminate barriers on the home front so they could join the exercise without compromising their manufacturing plant's results.

Leadership Principles

1. Conflict shows true character.
2. Conflict is expected. Be prepared.
3. Don't be blinded by the pressures of the day.

Chapter 22

Intentional Inclusion

> **Power Scripture:**
>
> *You shall not wrong one another, but you shall fear your God [with profound reverence]; for I am the Lord your God.*
>
> *Leviticus 25:17 (AMP)*

Inclusive Leadership

A critical trait of a great leader is inclusive leadership. This is the ability to lead a diverse organization in a way that values the uniqueness of skills, thoughts, approaches, styles, and experiences. It is making sure everyone is empowered and that an organization plays to individuals' strengths.

Inclusive leadership is not easy. It requires self-confidence to trust your judgments and to know you are doing the right thing. It requires a high level of emotional intelligence to understand and manage your emotions and those of others. Inclusive leadership also requires courage and constant effort to ensure that diversity of thoughts and input are sought after, valued, and respected.

To be an inclusive leader, you must be aware of your own biases and understand the power of diversity and inclusion to bring additional perspectives and input, with the benefit of strengthening your decision-making. Cultural intelligence and collaboration are traits that will enable an inclusive leader to be successful.

Inclusive leaders value, proactively seek out, and include diverse input into their plans. Inclusive leadership is intentional and requires you to understand how different people interact and communicate to be able to get everyone on the same sheet of music. Leaders very often develop that skill after a ground swell from an unhealthy environment, as was the situation I experienced.

I had just completed an assignment at one of our other locations, where I had been blessed with great success in my results. I already had a couple promotions under my belt in P&G and returned to Cincinnati with a new spirit, feeling empowered and ready to share my talents. I was enjoying the new challenges and envisioned unparalleled success. That was before I ran headlong into the reality that I was on a chess board of a white man's game playing by their rules.

The empowerment I took for granted at the other location was just a figment of my imagination at the technical center. We had gone through a rigorous training on diversity and inclusion at that site. I quickly realized that the same rigor had not been applied at this location.

When I joined the organization, there was quite a sizable contingent of women and minorities. Over several months, I noticed a disturbing trend. The women and minorities were leaving my technical function and moving to other roles that were more work process and organizationally oriented than the core technical roles. Puzzled by the trend, I started investigating the issues to understand why all the women were leaving, and why my African American friends were moving to other jobs.

There was a support group that had been established for minorities that met monthly. My boss, Ralph, who was white, was the sponsor of that support group. He attended every meeting. I was excited to get to the next minority support group meeting, where I would bring up my concern, not for the team to discuss (we had been discussing it at lunch tables) but for the leader, my boss, to help us start developing a clear path to a solution.

At the meeting, I felt observant and wise and was sure my question would get a good conversation going. Confidently, I leaned forward in my seat, elbows on the conference table, bent my head slightly, and with a professional quizzical look asked, "Ralph, I have noticed many of our best technical members, who happen to be women and minorities, are leaving our function. I am sure you have noticed that also. What do you think we should be doing to help change that trend? If we don't, one day we will turn around to realize we have a very monochromatic organization!" *Wow! That was good!* I thought to myself.

Ralph looked straight at me without even a blink or a smile. "Kennedy, you are new here. This meeting is so that each one of us can share our own personal situation and request input from the team. It is not to address other people's concerns." He then turned to scan the rest of the participants and continued. "Also, as a principle, we agreed that we would not take any work out of this meeting."

I was puzzled and asked, "Would you mind if I ask, why is that? Don't we want to make life better for everyone and, collectively, work towards that?"

"Look," Ralph responded, clearly frustrated, "it is clear you have missed the intent of this meeting. Let's move on with the agenda, and you should connect with Eduardo (the only Hispanic in our group) to get properly onboarded to the team." That answer was unsatisfactory, and this became an agenda item for my next one-on-one with Ralph.

I had been very involved in the diversity and inclusion efforts at the other location. Therefore, I had a lot of data and a wealth of learnings I could share in *this* organization. "If you want to see the change you want, lead it," one of my mentors would say. So, I convinced Ralph I should lead the diversity support group meetings.

He accepted and asked me what he could do to help, to which I replied, "You're welcome to join us once a quarter. Monthly is too often. Let me free up some time on your calendar by asking you to join us once a quarter for the second half of the meeting. I believe it will help others speak more freely of their concerns." It was actually my way of clearing the meeting for us to discuss driving some real change.

Ralph quickly accepted my offer and said, "You know, Kennedy, the culture here is different from the location you came from, so please don't try to change things." His face twisted slightly as if he were trying to smile, but disgust came through instead.

A couple months later, our diversity support team had documented sufficient data to validate our position that our technical function women and minorities were being poorly rated, coached and encouraged to leave, and moved into roles outside the function. Every member in the support group was frustrated and felt unsupported. The worst part was that they felt they would experience retaliation if they complained. If you had high ambitions and wanted to be successful, you would have to move out. And to support that, there were very few who looked like us in executive positions. Those who stayed in the technical function moved into roles in technical documentation versus those in core technical roles like project management, technical leadership, project delivery, or project design.

We presented our observations to our sponsor. He refuted that the data showed a problem by explaining that the women were making choices that would better help them raise a family and that it seemed Blacks and Hispanics were having difficulty with the technical depth needed to compete with the other (white) managers.

After much discussion, Ralph agreed to get me on the agenda of the Technical Leadership Team (TLT), which was led by our technical director, Sam.

It was not long before I was added to the TLT's agenda that I met with them the following first Monday of the month, per their schedule. The information I shared was very well-received and welcomed, especially by the three women who were on the team. One woman was from the human resources department, while another one was at job band level with the other TLT members and was frequently used by our director to showcase our diversity. The third woman was my peer but had been added to the TLT as a substitute for her manager, who was on a leave of absence. Our director thanked me for the information and dismissed me. Because my last slide of the presentation was a request for our diversity support group to meet with the TLT, I asked when they would get back to me on our request. The HR leader said she would work with the team schedule and get back to me. I left the conference room excited and feeling accomplished.

Later that day, Sam walked into my office. This was his first time stepping into my office. "Do you have a minute, Kennedy?"

"Oh, hi! Sure, Sam."

He closed the door and said, "When Ralph told me you were taking over the diversity support group, I thought it was a good use of your people skills. Now I'm thinking it was a bad mistake. You should focus your attention on delivering results versus worrying about other people's problems."

I knew what he was referring to, so I responded, "The support group meetings are during our lunch breaks, and there is no work at all. Any work we do is outside our normal work hours."

His response sounded as irrational as the game I decided to play. "If you are working one hundred and twenty percent, it should be all on your technical work-not that group."

I'm sure this was a game I should not have been playing, but it was too much fun. So, smiling and looking excited, I said, "Actually, with my workload, I am giving my job one hundred and twenty percent, but I also added another five percent to give to the organizational work."

Sam looked me straight in my eyes and said, "Then one hundred and twenty-five percent should all be on technical." His firm tone and volcanic look conveyed an even stronger message.

He was my boss's boss. The game was fun but dangerous, and it was one I could not win. My pushback ended there. I did not respond. My smile was stripped away.

As if by an act of grace, he said, "Here's what we are going to do. My team [TLT] will meet with your group. The only time I have available is this Friday at 5:00 pm. After that meeting, in exchange, you must promise me you will no longer lead this team or any of its efforts." Sam opened the door to leave but turned around and continued, "And so you don't cause any more confusion, I need you to keep this discussion between us. We have enough work and don't need to be distracted by your cause."

Sam really was not asking for a promise. He was giving me a directive.

That night, I drafted an invitation to go out to the women and minorities in the technical organization. The next morning, my administrative assistant typed it up and distributed the invitation to all thirty-two women and minorities in our technical organization across multiple locations in Cincinnati. I was inviting them to an Affirmative Action discussion (as it was referred to back then) with the TLT on Friday at 5:00 pm. It was Tuesday. Back then, digital social media was just a dream, so I started working the phones to explain what the meeting was about. I only had to explain it to the first five people, because the network took over and the word spread like wildfire - though not as fast as Twitter today!

That Friday by 4:00 pm, there were thirty-five participants present. This was one hundred percent turnout, plus three African American summer interns I did not know about. In my invitation, I had asked for them to show up at 4:00 pm so that we could take a few minutes to get on the same page and for me to share the background and answer any questions before the meeting. I left no room for confusion or chaos. The attendance by every member demonstrated how important that meeting was and how ready the diverse group was to be heard and to see change.

The meeting with the TLT was a rousing success. It met every objective I had. There were a lot of tears, as those present shared their feelings and pent-up frustrations. I remember, very clearly, the first Hispanic male in the technical organization giving his personal account. He was very tenured and did great work but was basically placed in a corner. At the end, some members of the TLT offered to join forces with us to help improve the work environment. One TLT member took over facilitation to create an action plan. Another facilitated the creation of sub teams to drive each action leg. Then, everyone looked at me to lead the execution plan moving forward. I could not. That was a very awkward situation for me, but I could not. Ralph, whom I am sure knew of my directive from Sam, then jumped in to rescue me. He shared that it would not be possible for me to lead and recommended someone else.

Over the next year, the technical organization started seeing some solid improvements in retention of our women and minorities, especially after the creative application of a safety tool, the Behavior Observation System. It's a tool where someone's behavior is observed in a particular action or interaction by an observer. That individual is then given feedback by the observer on his or her behavior. In this case, it was applied to behavior towards women and minorities. I may have had something to do with the creation of that tool based on my previous health and personal safety role. But neither my boss nor my director knew that I had designed and implemented it. I walk in the scripture that says, *"Do not withhold good from those to whom it is due [its rightful recipients], When it is in your power to do it." Proverbs 3:27 (AMP).*

God's Grace

Following the Affirmative Action meeting with the TLT, I came very close to accepting an offer with another Fortune 500 company and moving to Atlanta. One of my sponsors intervened and made me realize I would have left not because I hated my job or my great company but because of one man, Sam. On top of that, even the HR leader became a "protector" of my results from blatant retaliation. Doors opened to me as other leaders on the TLT recognized the shift I influenced. Leaders whom I had not interacted with in the past started asking for my input and thoughts on their diversity efforts. This gave me increased positive visibility. These were all favors my God poured on me.

Leadership Principles

1. Inclusive leadership is intentional and takes courage.
2. Leaders make a difference.
3. Be willing to do what others will not.

Chapter 23

Keep Rising

Career Management

If you are not being challenged but you want to progress and grow, then it's time for a change. It is imperative you manage your career to help you grow and increase your value. This, in turn, positions you to contribute even more, thereby increasing your return to your business. And no one can manage your career like you can.

You must be clear on what ultimate success looks like for you. This helps you stay focused on what progression is for you. It could be upwards or lateral. Lack of clarity will cause you to wander from one skill acquisition to the next without any apparent structure or end goal. The outcome will be that although you will have a surface knowledge of many areas, you will most likely have no technical depth in any. Managing your career also demands that you are clear on what choices you are willing or not willing to make to achieve the next milestone in your career. Critical to those choices is your work-life balance.

Personally, assess your growth and contributions to determine if a change is needed. What does not change gets left behind. In my situation below, I was extremely busy, but one day I realized I was bored from handling the same challenges, and the solutions were, in most cases, predictable. I woke up and realized I had settled too comfortably.

I have a rule of thumb: When I stop growing and can do a job in my sleep, or when I can do my manager's job better than I think he/she can, it's time for a change. It means I need to move forward to avoid stagnation, frustration, or contribution slippage. I found myself in such a situation while leading one of the largest groups with the biggest portfolio in my area of the business.

I had developed a solid portfolio of results by the halfway point in my career. My influence was global and beyond my scope of responsibilities. Added to that, my manager was not actively seeking to promote me; instead, he continued to increase my responsibilities while I continued to function without the position (of the next job band level).

I was doing a lot, but I could hear my mentor speaking in my head: "Don't ever confuse activities with achievements." It felt like I had a perpetual list of activities, and the results, although they were good for the business, were becoming less competitive, versus that of my peers.

I tapped into my internal network to uncover a few new assignment options. This all meant a move with several changes to deal with: my location, the technology I was familiar with, and the organization I loved, to name a few.

I pursued a potential assignment opportunity, which seemed the most exciting but not too challenging. It involved systems and processes, which were familiar to me, allowing me to minimize the number of personal changes I would be making. My drive was for a vertical startup in the new job in order to maximize my contributions, achieve top rating, and be positioned for the next career level within a couple of years.

With the help of a sponsor, I was able to gain an interview for the job. Other than my resume, all odds were stacked against me in this competitive environment. For starters, no one in that business knew much about me other than the high-level information they had from internal networking efforts I was involved in. I was also trying to fit into a culture that was very "family-oriented." I was coming from a large part of the business that some viewed as massive and arrogant. That perspective may have been correct, considering I really thought they needed me to come in and "save the day" with the work processes that had brought success to my old business. I was ready for the interview and was carrying my data to share on the superior results I had consistently delivered.

My plan was aborted at the beginning of the interview. Within the first two minutes of the welcome and introductions by Sandra, the manager, I threw my script out the door. This was not going to go as I had planned. It started differently. The welcome was more like a family reunion with members I had not met before. I was being treated like a family member. It was clear all their actions were not driven by politics and favoritism. Point one in favor of the job.

Next, Tom, one of my two interviewers, was at the same job band level as me. This told me that power was shared and not hugged by the manager. Point two for the job.

Then someone, looking very important and larger than life, interrupted us by entering the room with a huge smile, shook my hand firmly, and said, "Good luck on your interview. They need all the best help they can get because the business is growing." And she was gone . . . all in about ten seconds.

"Who was this whirlwind?" I asked.

"Oh, that's Beverly, our Vice President," was the response from Sandra. Point three for the job and, at that point, I knew this is where I wanted to be. This ten-second interruption told me upper leadership did not act like gods, as they were where I would be moving from.

The interview was going great. Then I felt the gulp in my throat when Tom looked at Sandra and said, "I think you are right. This is not going to work."

"Wait! What's not going to work?" I asked, puzzled. I felt like the process was ending before I even had a chance.

"The job you applied for," Sandra said. "You are very professionally qualified. However, Tom and I believe we have a bigger and better opportunity that has not yet been announced for which you have all the unique qualities to be our best candidate. It is a bigger job, but based on your past contributions, we believe you would take it beyond our vision and exceed our expectations." Talk about a vote of confidence - sold! When you have the favor of God in your life, blessings will come your way without you seeking them.

Several years later, after my promotion, I reflected on how God had pushed me out of my comfortable nest and steered me to where I was valued, recognized, appreciated, and rewarded, even before I had started the new role.

God's Grace

Before setting out to look for a new opportunity, I prayed and asked God to guide my footsteps to where and when he wanted me to go and to close doors that I should not enter. I also asked God to not make any suggestions but rather to hit me with a piece of 2 × 4 mahogany wood upside my head to make sure I saw what He had for me. I would not have landed this blessing if I had not stepped out in faith. He gave me favor with my interviewers, and He blessed me with something bigger and better than what I had left behind or was going after.

Leadership Principles

1. When you stop growing, it's time for a change.
2. The leader who does not change gets left behind.
3. Be better tomorrow than you are today.

Chapter 24

Your Next Chapter

Power Scripture:

"For I know the plans I have for you," declares the Lord, "plans to prosper you and not to harm you, plans to give you hope and a future."

Jeremiah 29:11 (NIV)

Transition

Transition in life is inevitable. We move from one situation to another. As leaders, our ability to handle transitions well will help us coach others going through what can be a traumatic experience. Having a plan of action makes complex transitions more manageable. Seeing a transition as an opportunity also makes it more welcoming.

Strong leaders face transition as an opportunity. These leaders are also change masters. It is an opportunity for growth and new beginnings. Embracing a change makes the transition more manageable and allows you to better define the path forward. It is amazing the number of leaders who neither have the ability to "let go" of the past easily nor embrace the future with great expectancy.

There are many transition models a leader can learn from. However, one of the key principles is *do not burn your bridges*. This means shut the door (of the old position) with excellence. In other words, leave the environment better than you met it. Go the extra mile to ensure, within your power, that your successor is well-positioned for a successful start. Also, don't forget to take the time to celebrate your successes before diving into another adventure. This paves the way for you to begin writing your new chapter, starting with a transition plan. Having a plan ensures control and intentional actions through the transition, rendering it seamless. If you have a learning orientation, it will help you build a solid foundation on your new path.

Sometimes, we are driven to a transition. Other times, we create the transition. The best way to predict the future is to create it. Self-awareness is important to help you determine when it is time to transition into another phase, as I did below during my last assignment with the best company (of people) anyone could be associated with: the Procter & Gamble Company.

My manager, Beverly, asked me to lead an urgent initiative, which involved migrating our business further into the digital age by moving systems and work processes into a new digital platform called Trafalgar. This would be a quick, twelve-month project. The request came halfway through the assignment I was enjoying and delivering solid results on.

"Beverly, are you seriously asking me to lead this work on top of what I am doing?" I asked.

"No. Of course not," Beverly replied. "I'm not that crazy. Your current work would transition to someone else because you will need focused attention to that project."

"Well, you know how great the results are that I'm delivering here. Would you not want me to see it through some better transition point?" I asked. "And oh, by the way, I have never worked in this field before that you are asking me to lead."

"Kennedy," she said firmly, "new and challenging things have not stopped you before. However, let me ask you. We have a critical need. This is a company-wide project that has been going on for several months, and our business is only now getting involved. I need someone who has experience in both of my business categories, someone who has strong project management and engineering skills, someone who is a strong collaborator, a leader who is not afraid of change and can manage up. Whom, would you say, are my best candidates to meet those criteria?"

I thought for a moment. No one came to mind, except . . . I was staring into a mirror. Beverly saw the contortion on my face, as it was obvious the light bulb went on, and I gave up.

"So, how can I find out more about the project?" I asked. Beverly was one of those managers you wanted to follow. She was a leader to whom you said, "yes" because you wanted to.

Soon after starting, it became clear to me that this would take twice as long as the twelve months expected and take me into one year of my protected timeline of three years to start the career of my dreams: retirement. It was not difficult to align my leadership and other relevant stakeholders with the new, realistic schedule. My team was able to lay the foundation for success with a solid plan to deliver on the new schedule. By the end of that first year, I lifted my head from being engulfed with the technical challenges, political hurdles, and schedule drivers to the realization that my work environment had changed far more than I'd realized.

I was moving to my third manager - in twelve months. Quite unusual for me. One of my new leaders had a conflicting leadership style to mine. Added to that new dynamic, I was feeling stifled by another leader in the organization, who'd had a track record of demonstrating a need for remedial training on styles and unconscious bias. I felt like an Oreo cookie, stuck between two managers who appeared to need help on being great leaders. My observation suggested that what made me the most successful in my career was being eroded. It was the empowerment to drive transformational change in process technologies and organizations. It was clear in my present situation that my cheese (motivation) had moved . . . or was moving!

After a review of our financial plan and dreams, my wife and I met with our financial advisor to complete the picture of our financial future. We then activated our planned actions for a smooth transition to life beyond corporate America.

One day, I looked to my wife to wake me from the dream and remind me that I needed to appreciate my job and be a good soldier. She looked at me and said, "Don't look at me. I'm retired, and I've been waiting for you to retire for a couple years now. God and I have already talked. We are just waiting on you to catch up!"

Okay, God, I got it. I met with my manager to inform her of my intent to retire in 12 months. That allowed me to complete my commitment to deliver the project successfully. A couple months later, it became official that I would be retiring after more than 30 years of service with one of the world's most amazing companies, Procter & Gamble.

God's Grace

God orchestrated my move to this assignment because He knew it was the final path for me to walk. He made the leadership changes that would allow me to step outside my comfort zone. This allowed me to retire comfortably - ahead of schedule and on my own terms.

"But remember the Lord your God, for it is he who gives you the ability to produce wealth, and so confirms his covenant, which he swore to your ancestors, as it is today." Deuteronomy 8:18 (NIV)

I always ask God to guide my footsteps. And He has, and He continues to do just that. His favor on my life led me to a point that I could comfortably transition to the next chapter of my life. He opened my eyes to observe the uncertainty in the environment and proactively initiated my transition at an ideal time. I ended that chapter while delivering significant results to our company and, at the same time, having more fun than I deserved. I then started the transition, having much to look forward to with the most wonderful life partner.

Leadership Principles

1. Transition in life is inevitable.
2. The best way to predict your future is to create it.
3. Great opportunities will pass if you get too comfortable for too long.

In Closing

Far greater than being a great leader is being a child of God. *Proverbs 8:35 (AMP) says, "For whoever finds me (Wisdom) finds life And obtains favor and grace from the Lord."*

You can also read, "For God so loved the world that he gave his one and only Son, that whoever believes in him shall not perish but have eternal life." John 3:16 (NIV)

If you don't know Jesus as your personal Lord and Savior, you can change that right here and right now. Just say the following prayer, and mean it in your heart:

Heavenly Father,

I acknowledge that I am a sinner.
I believe that Jesus died and rose
again for my sins. Your Word says in
John 3:16 that You love me so much
that You sent Your Son to die for my sins.

I ask You to please forgive me for my sins.

I accept Jesus as my personal Savior.

You also said that if I confess You with

my mouth and believe in my heart that

I will be saved. Thank you, Jesus, for saving me.

In Jesus' name. Amen.

If you prayed that prayer sincerely, that's all it takes to have Jesus in your life. Angels are now celebrating in Heaven! I encourage you to share your good news with someone else and find a good Bible-teaching church in your area to help you grow in Christ. Finally, all the instructions you need to walk with Jesus are found in His Book, The Bible.

How to Demonstrate

Effective Leadership Model

**LEADING WITH
YOUR HEART**

Care For Others
Become An Advocate
Create Harmony, Build Bridges
Sharing Wisdom, A Listening Heart
Your Word is Gold

**LEADING WITH
YOUR HANDS**

Enabling Success
Take Actions, Excellence
Be Courageous, Barrier-Buster
Progress-Focussed,
The Difficult Decision

**GREAT
LEADERS**

**LEADING WITH
YOUR HEAD**

It's Not Personal
Mountain-Mover
Unapologetically Confident
Speak Up, International Inclusion
A Super Vision, What Matters Most
No Dead Bodies, Your Next Chapter
Keep Rising

Questions for You to Reflect on and Discuss

1. Do you have to like someone or agree with their position to have a good business relationship with them?

2. What would you do if you witnessed bias against a colleague today?

3. How could you leverage individual sponsorship as a succession planning tool?

4. Why is it important that you get the culture right in the beginning of any new entity (team, group, organization)?

5. Would you give up your integrity for a business success if no one was watching? Why or why not?

6. As a mentor, what are the benefits of mentoring others?

7. Do you have to be a touchy-feely person to be empathetic to others? Why or why not?

8. At what point would you confront your peer or manager if they were not taking the time to do the job right?

9. How do you prepare yourself to make a controversial or difficult decision?

10. What are three things you can do to further empower your team that you have not done?

11. When do you determine a risk level is too high to take?

12. Do you agree with giving improvement feedback to hierarchy?

13. How do you balance when a solution is "good enough"?

14. Why is it important for you to involve the critics in helping you find a solution to a difficult problem?

15. What do you do to incite excitement for your vision?

16. How does others' trust in you increase your influence?

17. What did you do that was right, and what did you do that was wrong, when you felt personally attacked at work?

18. Write your top four priorities in order. How hard or easy can it be to protect your top priority?

19. What is the difference between confidence and arrogance?

20. How do you know you are communicating versus just speaking?

21. Was there a time you felt like a "dead body" after the implementation of an activity?

22. What do you think is a business case for inclusion?

23. How do you evaluate your personal development?

24. What are some indicators you saw that prompted your last transition?

Situational Application

Every personal experience is different. As a leader employing situational leadership styles, you flex your response to be appropriate to the situation. However, sometimes you just need a reminder, a memory-jogger, or something to jumpstart your thoughts and approach. Use this guide as jumper cables to help you sharpen your response to different situations.

	If you are in this situation	**Go to Chapter**
1.	Trying to build or strengthen a difficult business relationship:	*Build Bridges*
2.	Faced with injustice in the workplace:	*Care for Others*
3.	Concerned about advocacy:	*Become an Advocate*
4.	Dealing with a non-collaborative team:	*Create Harmony*
5.	Increasing your sensitivity to other cultures:	*Your Word is Gold*

6. Not sure you can be a good mentor: *Sharing Wisdom*

7. Dealing with a work member or team who is hurting: *A Listening Heart*

8. In a situation where someone is not pulling their weight: *Excellence*

9. Have a difficult or controversial decision to make: *The Difficult Decision*

10. Needing to drive a culture change: *Enabling Success*

11. Against the wall to deliver: *Take Action*

12. Need to delicately give feedback to hierarchy: *Be Courageous*

13. Progress is stalled, you're spinning your wheels, or dealing with a perfectionist: *Progress-Focused*

14. Facing a difficult problem to solve: *Barrier-Buster*

15. Have a vision, but no one else is excited about it—yet: *A Super Vision*

16. Need to change the course of a fast-moving team: *Mountain-Mover*

17. Dealing with peer hostility at work: *It's Not Personal*

18. Dealing with competing priorities: *What Matters Most*

19. Your capability is being questioned unjustly: *Unapologetically Confident*

20. Trying to execute your job in the face of resistance: *Speak Up*

21. Dealing with conflict: *No Dead Bodies*

22. Dealing with discrimination: *Intentional Inclusion*

23. Not feeling valued anymore: *Keep Rising*

24. Need to plan your next move: *Your Next Chapter*

My Favorite Dozen Leadership Principles

1. Invest in the development of relationships.

2. People need to know that you care before they care what you know.

3. The culture of an organization is a reflection of the leader.

4. Stop. Sit. Listen to your employees.

5. Real leadership starts with the heart.

6. Inspire an organization, and they will move mountains to deliver for the business.

7. Have a tolerance for and deal with uncertainty proactively.

8. Win with what really matters.

9. Self-confident leaders do not let others' emotional instability cause them undue stress.

10. Never settle for mediocrity in the name of efficiency.

11. The leader who does not change gets left behind.

12. The best way to predict your future is to create it.

References

1. *Oxford English Dictionary.* 3rd ed. Oxford: Oxford University Press. Continually updated at http://www.oed.com/, s.v. "grace."

2. *The Amplified Bible: Containing the Amplified Old Testament and the Amplified New Testament.* La Habra, CA: The Lockman Foundation, 2015.

3. Peterson, Eugene H. *The Message: The Bible in Contemporary Language.* Carol Stream, IL: NavPress, 2005.

4. Ray, John. *A Collection of English Proverbs Digested into a Convenient Method for the Speedy Finding Anyone Upon Occasion; with Short Annotations. Whereunto are Added Local Proverbs with Their Explications, Old Proverbial Rhythmes, Less Known or Exotic Proverbial Sentences, and Scottish Proverbs.* Cambridge [Cambridgeshire]: Printed by John Hayes, 1670.

5. *The Holy Bible: English Standard Version.* Wheaton, IL: Good News Publishers, 2001.

6. *Holy Bible: New International Version.* Grand Rapids, MI: Zondervan, 1985.

Notes

Chapter 2:

1. "Freedom comes with excellence"; Adapted from the Hindu saying, "With Freedom comes responsibility."

2. "People need to know that you care before they care what you know." (Adaptation from Theodore Roosevelt)

3. "Never confuse activity with achievement." (John Wooden)

Chapter 5:

1. A.G. Lafley was Procter & Gamble Chairman, President and CEO from 2000–2010, 2013–2015.

Chapter 7:

1. Richard Deupree was the first individual to be named Procter & Gamble President and Chairman of its Board who was not from the Procter or the Gamble families. 1930–1948.

Chapter 8:

1. "In God we trust. All others must bring data." (W. Edwards Deming)

2. "Opportunity is missed by most people because it is dressed in overalls and looks like work." (Thomas Edison)

Chapter 12:

1. "Efforts and courage are not enough without purpose and direction." (John F. Kennedy, 35th US President)

Chapter 13:

1. "78% Done Is Better Than 100% Perfect." There is nothing magical about the number "78." I used it intentionally to generate the conversation versus blanket acceptance or rejection of the idea of moving forward with what is "good enough."

2. "You will make more progress when you add data to emotions." (Author Unknown).

Chapter 14:

1. "If you stay with the problem long enough to understand it, the solution will present itself." (Albert Einstein)

Chapter 15:

1. "If you don't have a vision of where you want to go, any road will take you there." (Lewis Carroll

Chapter 16:

1. "Mastery earns you the right to be able to influence." (Anonymous)

Chapter 17:

1. "If you are a leader and no one is following, you are just out for a walk." (Afghan proverb)

Chapter 20:

1. "Anything worth doing is worth doing right." (Hunter S. Thompson)

Chapter 22:

1. "If you want to see the change you want, lead it." (Mahatma Gandhi)

Chapter 24:

1. "Know when your cheese has moved." (Adapted from "Who Moved My Cheese?" Spencer Johnson, MD, 1998)

2. "The best way to predict your future is to create it." (Abraham Lincoln)

About the Author

Kennedy A. Germain retired after a successful career of more than thirty years at Procter & Gamble, the largest consumer goods company in the world. While at P&G, Kennedy gained extensive leadership experience in several of the businesses across multiple locations at P&G's technical centers and manufacturing plants.

Kennedy is from the Caribbean Island nation of Dominica, affectionately referred to as The Nature Island. He is a graduate of Tuskegee University. He is also a poet and a photographer. Kennedy's first publication was a mini book of poetry, *As We Pondered*, which he co-authored with his high school friend Eddie Toulon.

Kennedy lives out his mission every day, which is, "To be a blessing to those I interact with and to make a positive difference in at least one person's life each day."

Kennedy and his wife, Junie, currently spend their time between Cincinnati, Ohio, and the Caribbean Island of Saint Lucia. They have two children and two grandchildren.

Also by Kennedy A. Germain

Germain Empowerment

If this book was a blessing to you, then you may be interested in subscribing to my leadership blog, where I share generally unconventional perspectives to empower every leader through relatively short, easy-to-read posts.

Be Empowered,
Kennedy A. Germain

Email: kennedy@germainempowerment.com

Website: https://germainempowerment.com

FREE eBook:
Stress Busters: The Other 5 Practical Steps Anyone Can Take

Scan the QR to download

Made in the USA
Middletown, DE
28 September 2022

11301272R00129